"Shawn writes from a place of passion, dedication, and a burning desire to always do better. His stories are both gripping and inspirational. They make you want to sling your backpack over your shoulder and head off for adventure."

— Ray Zahab
Adventurer, Ultramarathon Runner
Author, Founder of impossible2Possible

"*TEAMS ON THE EDGE* is a testament to how teams can be shaped, molded, and taught how to achieve incredible results. Through his gripping storytelling Shawn makes you feel like you're living the adventures alongside him and in the end the result is a transformed reader with a more thorough understanding of how to make teams better."

— Sami Jo Small
Canadian Olympic Hockey Goalie, 3-time Medallist
Author, Professional Speaker

"*TEAMS ON THE EDGE* is a great read and contains many valuable lessons for both wilderness and urban leaders. Each story drives home the importance of caring, competent leadership and the importance of building a strong team."

— TA Loeffler, PhD
Professor of Outdoor Recreation
at Memorial University of Newfoundland,
Author, Mountaineer

"Great read. Stratton paints a great picture of the NOLS instructor lifestyle: the good, bad, and ugly. Anyone who wants to be a NOLS instructor should read this book."

— Darran Wells
Associate Professor of Outdoor Education & Leadership
at Central Wyoming College, Senior NOLS Instructor,
Author of *NOLS Wilderness Navigation*

TEAMS ON THE EDGE

STORIES & LESSONS FROM WILDERNESS EXPEDITIONS

SHAWN STRATTON

FORMER NATIONAL OUTDOOR LEADERSHIP SCHOOL INSTRUCTOR

Published in Canada by Greens Pond Publishing
Suite 110, 38 Pearson Street
St. John's, NL, Canada, A1A 3R1

Library and Archives Canada Cataloguing in Publication

Stratton, Shawn, 1974-

    Teams on the edge: stories and lessons from wilderness expeditions / author, Shawn Stratton; editors, Clare-Marie Grigg, Casey Livingston, Iona Bulgin; cover and book layout, Jen Moss.

Short stories.
Issued also in an electronic format.
ISBN 978-0-9917409-0-1

    I. Grigg, Clare-Marie II. Livingston, Casey III. Bulgin, Iona IV. Title.
PS8637.T737T42 2013   C813'.6   C2013-900738-5

e-book ISBN: 978-0-9917409-1-8

First Edition 2013, Printed in La Vergne, Tennessee, USA
Typeset in Minion, Bebas, and Frutiger
Cover Photo: Milam Valley, India. Shawn Stratton
Back Cover Photo: Unnamed Peak, Healy Mountains, Alaska. Shawn Stratton

For corporate inquiries and bulk orders, please contact
info@livemoregroup.com

Disclaimer

The National Outdoor Leadership School (NOLS) has neither endorsed, sponsored, nor authorized this publication. The views expressed herein are solely those of the author and do not necessarily represent the view of NOLS.

All the stories are true; all names and distinguishing characteristics have been changed.

Dedication

To **Stacie Farmer** (left) and **Cary Girod** (right), two of my NOLS students who were tragically killed in separate accidents by vehicles while riding their bikes just a few years after taking their course.

TEAMS ON THE EDGE:
TABLE OF CONTENTS

TEACHING IN A CLASSROOM
WITHOUT WALLS

It wouldn't be an adventure if you already knew the ending.

BEING AN OUTDOOR EDUCATION INSTRUCTOR is more of a life-style than a job. I was paid to travel the world for almost 15 years, leading glacier mountaineering, backpacking, sea kayaking, and white-water canoeing courses in far-flung locations around the globe. I was, as some might say, *living the dream*. I loved the job so much that, even though my yearly tax return said I was scraping by just above the poverty line, I felt rich. To make this life possible, I lived out of my little red Mazda truck. Everything I owned fit in the back, and there was room left for me to sleep. In nine years I didn't live in one place for more than three months. Three times I drove to Alaska, twice from Mexico. Now that's a commute!

When I look back over my years of leading wilderness expeditions, two particularly vivid memories jump to mind. The first is the sight of a rescue helicopter lifting off in a white wall of blowing snow from the side of a remote, storm-logged mountain. It's carrying one of my students with an injury so severe it could have meant loss of limb or fatal infection had the cloud cover not shifted for a few precious minutes, allowing it to land. The second image is of returning to camp after a short hike with a group on a three-month course canoeing a remote Alaskan Arctic river to find our tents and gear—our essential, life-sustaining supplies—shredded as if by a horde of malevolent beasts. Never before has my stomach plummeted so rapidly to my feet.

You'll notice both instances occurred in extremely remote locales. I find that every aspect of life and death is heightened in the wilderness. Friendships build faster when a team is pushed to the edge of its comfort zone; sunrises are more stunning; vistas are more awe-inspiring; camp food tastes richer. And danger looms larger. A twisted ankle is not so simple when the mobility of the team is compromised; rescue becomes death-defying in itself. Teams under pressure is a consistent theme throughout this collection of adventure stories. It's amazing how magnified the highs and lows of life become when they unfold in the middle of the wilderness.

Another theme, and the most significant for me, is the importance of a team. More than anything, these flashbacks underscore the power of teams. As a leader, I look back proudly on those two challenges. Each event could have ended disastrously, but the cooperation, commitment, and high level of communication among the members of the group not only surmounted calamity but also allowed both teams to strengthen and both expeditions to excel.

I decided to write this book about some of my real-life stories because I feel there are many lessons to be shared from these experiences. I'm extremely proud of the teams I've led. We began each adventure as a group of assembled individuals; we walked out of the wilderness as a team. The details behind the entertaining and sometimes scary stories of overcoming misadventure, life-threatening accidents, challenging decision-making, and disgruntled team members are the elements that gelled each group into a fine team. Dealing with these experiences has left a lasting impression on me and taught me lessons worth sharing.

Why NOLS?

All of the stories recorded here were either National Outdoor Leadership School (NOLS) expeditions or were made possible through NOLS funding.

NOLS teaches wilderness skills and leadership for the purposes of both educating people and serving the environment. Most of the participants are American college students looking to earn extra credits in a more unusual and interesting way than traditional classroom lectures. Most are also hoping for an unforgettable, life-changing experience. Some students even hope to become instructors one day.

I was a young man when I first learned about NOLS in an Adventure-Based Experiential Education class in college in 1995. I nodded my head as I sat at the desk, thinking *I'll work there some day*. After several years pondering careers, that night the light bulb had been turned on in my head. I called NOLS headquarters the next morning, requested a catalogue, and devoured every page when it arrived. From that day on I became enthralled with everything NOLS.

Growing up in Newfoundland, Canada, an island in the North Atlantic Ocean and North America's most easterly point, I'd never been exposed to the world of outdoor education and my family was not interested in camping. Yet, as a youngster, I always loved adventure and, fortunately, thanks to the Scouts, I was able to develop my passion for the wilderness. I was 20 years old in the fall of 1995 when I learned about NOLS. I spent the next four years building my resume so that I could eventually apply for an Instructor Course. I took the Instructor Course in the spring of 1999. At 24, I was the second youngest person in the course; the average age was 28.

Becoming an instructor with NOLS is no small test of will. From the beginning, an applicant has to go through a highly competitive selection process toward being accepted into a 35-day course (also referred to as the 35-day interview). You must be prepared to relinquish a month of your life, as well as pay for the opportunity, which promises in-depth instruction on NOLS protocol and the NOLS curriculum. However, being accepted and taking part doesn't guarantee you a job. Most businesses would doubtless love to have a testing period for their potential new hires, but most people would never agree to endure it, let alone pay for it. The fact that potential employees are willing to pay and take the Instructor Course is a testimony to the unflinching desire people have to work for NOLS.

I'll never forget the day I got the call. I was backpacking on my own around New Zealand, when I called home to check in with my family. My mother relayed the good news that I'd been selected from the wait list to take part in the Instructor Course starting in just two weeks in Tucson, Arizona. Despite the fact that this was my dream, I had a tough time deciding whether I should accept. I had planned to stay in New Zealand for another month and hadn't yet made it to the part of the country I most wanted to visit: the Southern Alps. When I got the news, I was in the remote mountain highway village of Arthur's Pass, and I had no idea how I'd get to Tucson within two weeks, much less generate the money to pay for the course. I'd saved to buy an open ticket to return to Canada and had roughly $500 to my name. I couldn't easily buy a ticket to Tucson, let alone pay for the course; I was working my way around New Zealand, just making enough money to keep traveling on a tight budget.

NOLS also told me that, if I passed, they would immediately offer me two summer contracts, which is rare, but they were short-staffed that year. I needed to be available to work for them if I were to take the course. Problem was, I'd already committed to work for another company, doing a multi-adventure teen expedition in Alaska. I hated having to let this company down, as I'd worked for them before and they'd given me an amazing reference. I had just two hours to make the decision or someone else would be offered my spot.

With no idea how I was going to make it happen, I said, "Yes!"

Of course. It was my dream job.

I just hoped everything would work out. Through the jigs and the reels (a Newfoundland expression!), it did. I found solutions to all the obstacles and made it to Tucson on time. Having gone through considerable upheaval to get to the Instructor Course, I placed tremendous pressure on myself to do well and pass. Unfortunately, it turned out to be the worst outdoor education experience of my life, and it nearly turned me off ever working in the industry again, let alone working for NOLS.

From the beginning of the course I just wasn't myself. Having never taken a regular NOLS student course before and not knowing anyone else who had, I was fairly green, unlike many other applicants. From the first day, when I accidentally burned the hash browns, I grew more and more nervous. I'd find myself having internal pep talks, *Relax, you know this stuff and deserve to be here.* After the first few days we shared our personal goals with the group and all I could blurt out was, "I just don't want to fuck up!" Nearly all the other instructor candidates had either taken a NOLS student course or worked for NOLS in a support role. They were much more familiar with the NOLS style of camping and what an Instructor Course was *really* like.

From then on the "interview" kicked into high gear, and it was almost a competition among the candidates to see who could impress the instructors the most. It turned out that this was not "staff training" and they actually wanted us to behave as students. This wasn't a stretch for most people on the course because many had been NOLS students previously, but I'd been leading expeditions for four years and hadn't been a student in a long time.

Upon completion of the course, students are evaluated and ranked in order of most-ready-to-work. Even if they are cleared to work, it can take a year or two for new instructors to be assigned their first expedition. Some participants are deemed not ready to work and are asked to attain further training or are discouraged from working for the school altogether. I was devastated when I was told that I was one of the few who needed more training. When I was given the news, it was—and still is—one of the most gut-wrenching moments of my life. I was told I didn't have enough off-trail navigational skills to work as a NOLS instructor. It was upsetting news to me because even though (granted) my group *did* veer off course on one of the last days during the hiking section, I was confident in my off-trail navigation. Making it even more tough to take, it seemed I'd only just missed out on being accepted, because the rest of my evaluation was strong: I had a talent for working in outdoor education and was close to being an instructor. Despite the rough experience and the devastation of rejection, I felt a certainty that I had the talent, passion, and drive to be a worthy NOLS instructor some day soon.

So I persevered.

After discussing the next course of action open to me with NOLS staff, I took a shorter instructors' seminar later that summer. It was a backpacking course offered to NOLS paddling instructors and I was determined to prove that my navigation skills were up to snuff. As it happened, the senior instructor leading the trip had no issue with my abilities and said he was surprised I hadn't passed my Instructor Course. He spoke with the NOLS staffing office and gave me approval to work field courses as an instructor.

My first course job (as a co-instructor, which is how everyone starts) came around the following summer. It was a Wind River mountain range backpacking course in Wyoming. When the course was finished, I knew that this was the job and company I wanted to work for. I loved the length (average, 27 days) and structure of NOLS expeditions; they gave you time to get to know the students and see them grow. I loved pushing students to the edge of their comfort zones daily and seeing them rewarded for their efforts.

Living the Dream

I discovered that I strongly related to teaching in a classroom without walls. In the NOLS environment, most of the learning is applied immediately, be it during glacier travel, through effective feedback, or in an outdoor cooking class. I'd tell most people who asked what I did for a living that I was a *mountain or sea kayak guide* because they rarely understood the term *outdoor educator*. NOLS instructors are educators, first and foremost. They teach students important leadership, natural history, risk management, and outdoor living skills, which they can use in college, at the office, at home, or on their own wilderness expeditions. It's about helping people become comfortable with themselves, which in turn helps them become more positive, contributive members of society.

I thrived when I was challenged by harsh weather, difficult terrain, long days, and the occasional crisis. You'll read about several of those tough situations in the pages ahead. Although they make for good stories, I'm thankful that all my courses weren't quite so dramatic or before long I'd have been struck down with burnout or suffered a nervous breakdown! My goal in going to NOLS was to work as much as I could, in as many different course types and locations as possible. That's precisely what I did for nine years. As much as it was something like *living the dream*—and it was certainly living *my* dream—adventure travel is really only glamorous in retrospect. It involves very little pay and few benefits, constant low-budget travel, caring for and teaching people in remote and often harsh environments, weeks and months away from loved ones, and constant physical strain.

To put up with all these challenges, what did I get?

The privilege to play an integral part in a life-changing experience for my students. Many alumni call their NOLS adventure one of the greatest experiences of their lives. Not many people can say they were a part of something like that when they go to work each day.

An opportunity to be employed alongside incredibly gifted, dedicated, and inspiring people who work for the company because they believe in its mission.

A chance to get paid to see many of the most isolated and beautiful places in the world that even locals rarely get to see: remote waterfalls in the Kimberley outback of Australia, unclimbed peaks in the Indian Himalayas, pristine beaches in Mexico, and calving glaciers in Alaska.

Incredible road trips throughout North America. As mentioned earlier, I drove to Alaska three times, twice from Mexico and once from San Francisco.

The chance to live a life of adventure, not knowing how each day would play out, yet feeling reassured that I had the skills and experience I needed, as well as an outstanding team of professionals for support.

The opportunity to make decisions of consequence. When you're leading a course in the field, it's up to you and your co-instructors to make all the decisions. And one of those decisions could mean the difference between life and death.

And a great collection of stories to tell.

OVER THE EDGE

Photo: Dave Nathanson

CHAPTER 1

IT'S 3:30 P.M., DEEP IN THE HIMALAYAN MOUNTAIN RANGE *just west of India's second highest peak, Nanda Devi, and I'm standing with my co-instructor listening to a strange, moaning sound. It seems to be coming from the drainage area sloping 300 feet upward away from our campsite. At first I think students have hiked up to where the area narrows into a canyon and are fooling around, making echoes, but as I move toward the noise, it begins to resemble at one moment that of a drunken shepherd, the next, an injured wild animal. I start running, listening intently, and it suddenly dawns on me that what I'm hearing are bloodcurdling cries for help.*

It was day 28 of our NOLS expedition trekking through the Himalayas—the "Abode of Snow"—and the highest mountain range in the world. Our group, composed of twelve students, me, and two co-instructors, had been having the time of our lives. My co-instructors, Sameera and Rajan, were both from India and had also attended a NOLS Instructor Course in the United States. They were talented wilderness educators but had less experience working for NOLS than I had. Their depth of local knowledge and ability to speak the language made them a tremendous asset. Combined with my extensive NOLS experience, we were a well-balanced team. One of the things I most love about traveling the Himalayas in India and Nepal are the cultural experiences of passing through remote villages not accessible by vehicles.

Shawn capturing an image of the children in a remote village after playing kick ball. Pindari Valley, India. *Bryan Schmidt*

With most other mountain ranges in the world, you miss out on this opportunity because roads bypass communities and take you directly to the trailheads. Early on in our trip we'd been fortunate to hike through isolated communities, spending time in schools and with local families. We even stumbled into the thick of a huge, 10-foot-high marijuana field. Picture that: college students suddenly face-to-face with marijuana plants almost twice their size. Of course no one was allowed to test the local product, which is farmed as much for medicine and making rope, fencing, and other building materials as it is for recreational purposes. But there were certainly lots of faces buried in the foliage, endless photos taken, and no doubt later on, back home, several Facebook profile pictures updated.

As we climbed higher into the mountains, we came across beautiful shrines. They were a multicolored line upon line of bells, hanging as intentions of safe passage for the people who passed by. The tradition was that each time one of the bells was rung, it sent a prayer out into the wind. We had come prepared with a bell of our own, bearing all our names, which we hung up and rang many times.

Students checking out a marijuana plantation. Pindari Valley, India. *Shawn Stratton*

Before long we realized we could use those prayers. The trail became unusually challenging, with late monsoon rains causing landslides and washouts that at one point closed our intended route for 10 days, forcing us to go in the opposite direction. The team was forced to improvise. Several times we had to cross steep and exposed slopes where normally there would have been a four-foot-wide stone path. Although the towering mountains were wearing their ever-present caps of snow, it was only October and we had expected the valleys and pathways to remain clear. A little snow wouldn't have mattered, but we hadn't factored in such excessive rain. It was an ominous feeling to be heading deeper into the mountains as we passed other trekkers and shepherds heading out, telling us to turn around because the trails had been washed away.

But we weren't about to walk out on day seven of our 34-day section without first giving it an honest effort. The Himalayan Mountains provide just the sort of invigorating environment many wilderness lovers thrive on. It's a life-changing, character-building sort of trip, and with the right equipment, food, and techniques it can offer what I call "camping in style." Fortunately (or unfortunately), NOLS is probably the only company operating in the Indian Himalayas that doesn't use mules or porters to transport participants' equipment. Carrying our own gear (packs weighing 60 pounds) and being self-sufficient allowed us to travel over much more challenging terrain than mules and porters could usually manage. So we persevered.

With just six days left to go, we were nearing the end of our expedition. The students had just returned to camp after a four-hour solo hike and we were having a layover day. Our location was deep in the Shalang Valley at 12,000 feet, surrounded by 20,000-foot mountains, a long three-day walk from the nearest road. The ground cover was dotted with grassy tussocks and three-foot-high shrubs. The weather was cool and the sky overcast, shedding light snow flurries throughout the day. The previous night, a foot of snow had fallen, but it had melted away after a few hours.

Mike's Misstep

Around 3 p.m., Mike, one of the students, headed off to get water for his tent group from a nearby stream located 40 feet below a hard packed dirt slope. Tall and athletic, Mike was a popular, happy-go-lucky guy from New York. He had a thirst for adventure and had been doing well on the course.

He walked along the ridge above the stream, swinging his water bag and scoping out the area. He sprang up onto a small boulder, trying to determine the best way down: either a steep but quick, 35- to 45-degree direct route in front of him, or a less steep but more time-consuming route a few hundred yards away. As he stood half-pondering, half-enjoying his surroundings, the sodden ground beneath his feet, weary of being pummeled by rain, hail, and melted snow, suddenly made the decision for him. It crumbled loose, sending Mike's 200 pounds tumbling down a slope equivalent in steepness to a black diamond ski run.

Taken completely by surprise, Mike crashed into the stream as his left leg flailed across a rock, snapping in a way that, despite an odd absence of pain, he knew was bad. At the same time, several large rocks slithered down, striking him in the back, sending panicked thoughts of spinal injuries flying through his head.

At first, he just lay where he was, struggling for breath, afraid to move and risk further injury. But the water was icy and the unwelcome prospect of hypothermia began to beat out his other fears, so he slowly nudged his way out of the stream until he was half-sitting on a rock, his damaged leg still dragging in the water.

Shivering, Mike took a deep breath and clasped his left knee with both hands, pulling his leg closer. His rain pants were soaked through and ripped and he could make out a bleeding gash just below the knee. There was something sticking to the area and automatically he reached down to pull it away. It was small and hard and, as he picked it up, he felt he should know what it was, but his brain wouldn't kick in. Dazed, he dropped his hand and tried to rinse the object in the rushing water. When it suddenly slipped from his fingers and disappeared, he made the connection. It was a piece of bone. His bone. And he'd just washed it away. The enormity of the situation hit him like a truck. And he opened his mouth, drew air deep into his lungs, and screamed for help.

Ten minutes later, Mike was still yelling. His cries seemed to be swallowed up by the rushing water. Exhausted and clearly failing to attract his team's attention, he fell silent, suddenly focusing instead on how incredibly cold he felt. He tried to give himself a sternum rub to warm up his core, but this only worked momentarily. He was suddenly terrified that no one would hear him. No one would find him.

Time ticked on. He continued yelling and screaming as he shivered and stared longingly at the ridge above, willing someone to appear. The wind blew, sending mocking puffs of earth rolling down the slope and, still, there was no sign of life. He dropped his head, feeling utterly defeated and desperately alone. He started to lose hope.

Suddenly he heard something. It was a girl's voice calling his name. "Mike? Mike!" His head snapped up. It was Mary, one of his fellow students, standing like a savior at the top of the ridge.

"My Bone's Sticking Out of My Leg"

At around 3:30 p.m. I was taking notes in the instructor's tent when Janet, one of the students, rushed over. She said she and her friends could hear strange noises coming from the drainage area near camp.

"Is everyone *in* camp?" I asked.

"Yes… I think," she replied tentatively. I stood up and we rushed out of the tent, heading toward the stream. I stopped and listened. Janet was right. I could hear strange cries floating on the wind. The closer we got, the more urgent they became. And the more they sounded like panicked cries for help.

Minutes later we reached the edge of the slope. By this time, the cries had fallen silent. Several students who were already standing there clustered around us.

"Mike's down there," someone began to explain. "He's broken his leg. We thought he was just acting out a first-aid scenario at first, but Mary went down, all annoyed, to tell him it was too cold and it was about to start snowing and to give it up, but then I think he showed her his leg and it's broken. It's definitely broken."

It was as if time stopped. I took a deep breath and thought, *Oh boy, here we go*. Although I had more than 15 years of first-aid training, I'd never had to treat a broken bone, let alone treat one in such a remote and harsh environment. Thankfully, my brain clicked into crisis mode and, as if on automatic, my training took over. I quickly set the students to collecting splinting materials, sleeping bags, and sleeping pads. Fortunately, the team had recently finished a five-day wilderness advanced first-aid program as part of their semester.

As soon as I'd delegated jobs, I scoped out a safe route down the slope and carefully made my way toward Mike, who was in a semi-reclined position on a small rock beside Mary. When I reached him, his face looked ghostly pale behind his dark beard. He shivered, and smiled.

"Hey, Shawn," he quavered. The color had drained from his

face. My bone's sticking out of my leg."

Huh. *This guy's definitely in shock.*

I knew he must be in tremendous pain and, realizing that shock can be even more dangerous than a broken limb, I asked a student to get Rajan to bring the drug kit so I could administer some immediate relief.

Although obviously dazed, Mike appeared coherent and reliable and, in addition to his leg injury, which I still hadn't examined, was complaining of low right-sided back pain from being struck by rolling rocks. Deciding that possible spinal or internal injuries might be the more serious issue at hand, I first did a head-to-toe exam, starting with his back. He had some bruising, but I couldn't see any indication of other injuries, although I was worried about possible internal damage.

Rajan arrived with the drug kit and Mike was given a strong narcotic pain reliever. Other students had brought additional supplies by this point, so Rajan went back to camp to call Mandeep, the NOLS India program director, on the satellite phone to request a helicopter evacuation for a limb-threatening injury.

The team's first-aid training was now a significant asset. Mike was shivering and complaining of being cold, so before doing anything else, we carefully moved him in a seated position about 10 feet back from the stream. We then reclined him onto a sleeping pad, with his injured leg supported by more pads, and wrapped him in several sleeping bags. I asked Mary to sit by his head as a reassuring presence to comfort and distract him from any pain he might experience once we started working on his injury. Two students performed another thorough head-to-toe exam, measured vitals, and asked Mike key assessment questions about his injury. This was helpful because it allowed me to focus on the break itself. I had to take a moment before cutting away the material of Mike's pant leg because I knew what I was about to see would be gruesome, most likely the worst injury any of us had ever encountered. I picked up my scissors and carefully sliced through his sodden, blood-soaked Gore-Tex rain layer and then his fleece pants.

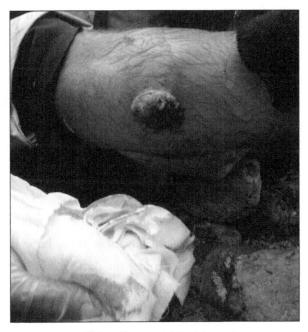

Mike's open fracture wound. *Dave Nathanson*

I peeled away the material and sat back to observe the large bloody gash. Strangely, my first thought was, *Oh, bones are grey.* I guess I'd been imagining white bone, like a chicken leg. The wound was a bad one: It was 2.5 inches in diameter. It looked as if the insides of Mike's leg were clamoring to force their way outside with the protruding bone, a mess of fatty tissue, muscle, and, of course, blood. There was an additional injury, a small puncture, closer to his knee, and several bleeding but minor abrasions.

We got straight to work. Something clicked in my head, like a parent jumping to the aid of a child in need. Surprisingly, I didn't feel scared or queasy; failure wasn't an option. I had to stabilize this injury and everything was going to work out fine. I'd trained for this kind of scenario for years, but I'd never had to use that training. I irrigated the wound with water from Mike's dromedary bag. Disinfected water wasn't immediately available and I wasn't willing to wait, so I made the call that at 12,000 feet the water from the nearby spring was clean enough. The wound, which had been covered up by the pant leg, appeared to be free of dirt and grit.

Next came the tricky and painful part. Mike was semi-comfortable, and his wounds were clean. It was time to apply traction in order to line up his shin with his ankle in the hope that the exposed bone would slide back under the skin. Our intent was to provide some pain relief in the long run, but this would likely be an excruciating procedure. Until now, Mike had been admirably self-possessed, brave, and strong. We knew he had to be in extreme pain, but we barely heard a whimper out of him. But even Mike bellowed like a bull moose when Sameera clasped his ankle and pulled with all her might to force his bone back into place. She gave it a considerable effort, but Mike's tibia stubbornly resisted. Seeing his terrible pain, we abandoned the exercise.

I set about treating the injury as an open wound, dressing it with three sterile gauze pads, wet to dry. The first pad was soaked in water and placed directly over the exposed wound, the second dampened lightly, and the third dry. I then wrapped the pads in place with gauze cling and treated the smaller abrasions with adhesive bandages. Suddenly I noticed a thick, two-inch cylinder of partially coagulated blood spurt from the puncture just below his knee. Up until then it had appeared blood-free, but it was as if by applying pressure to the main wound blood had been forced out through this other injury. I quickly cleaned and covered that area and then wrapped his entire lower leg, from knee to ankle, in a secure bandage. It was difficult to judge the tightness, so we kept monitoring the circulation in Mike's left foot.

By this time, around 4:15 p.m., the students had amassed a supply of splinting materials from the camp. I didn't want them using their own clothes in the splint. They still had another five days in the snowy mountains and we literally had only the clothes on our backs. Mike was already wearing nearly all his clothes (which, of course, he also needed) so I wasn't left with many items to use for insulation and padding. In the end, we splinted Mike's leg using his fleece vest and two foam half-pads. A sock was placed under his slightly bent knee and another sock with the toe cut off was taped around his foot to keep it warm. Two trekking poles, extending from mid thigh to several inches below his foot, were tied in place with cord from the tents. Both legs were then wrapped in a semi-inflated sleeping pad that was tied with cord and then inflated to make an improvised air cast. Mike would remain in this for the next 24 hours.

A Slippery Slope

Around 5 p.m., we prepared to carry Mike up the slope into a more comfortable, warmer environment. Students had moved a tent closer to the top of the drainage area to shorten the journey. But first we had to figure out how to hoist him safely up the crumbling incline. To get up and down the drainage area we'd used a less steep route than the one Mike had fallen down, but it was located 200 yards away, which seemed like a mile when faced with carrying a seriously injured six-foot, one-inch, 200-pound patient. Sameera and I considered the immediate, steeper, but also quicker route as a way out. We experimented with cutting steps into the hard packed earth with our ice axes. We had no rope and no time to make a stretcher with our packs, so we'd have to carry him as a human stretcher instead. I didn't think we could slog it out on the longer route. So with much consternation and feeling considerable stress about it, I made the call to haul him up the direct, steeper way.

By this time it was getting dark and only half of us in the drainage area had headlamps. The temperature was dropping, light snow was falling, and Mike, now paler, was still in shock. The sense of urgency to get him up the slope and into a warm tent was palpable. I organized the carry and, with Mike lying flat, I had people line up on either side and stretch their hands underneath him to grasp the hands of the person on the other side. Carrying Mike up the first 10 feet was slow, but relatively smooth. But a quarter of the way up, the route steepened and the hard packed dirt stopped giving traction and, even when chopped into steps, crumbled away. People on the uphill side of the carry were beginning to lose their footing, letting go of Mike as they slithered on their backs underneath him. I had terrifying visions of a tumbleweed of students cascading down the slope, but fortunately there were enough people so that when one tapped out, another could immediately take his or her place. We reached a point where we were moving one step at a time before strategically repositioning.

"Okay! We're going to do a step. One, two, THREE!"

I hadn't planned on being part of the human stretcher. Instead I would guide the group up the slope and chop steps where necessary, but, by now, I was also carrying Mike, after replacing an exhausted student. I was terrified of dropping him and of losing my own balance and getting hurt. My muscles felt as if they would snap; my toes clenched inside my boots as if to better cling to the earth. I could see the exertion on everyone's faces. Each member of the human stretcher pushed themselves closer to the breaking point, knowing that Mike was relying on them to act as a strong team unit. Less than 10 feet from the top, I suddenly doubted if we could make it. I didn't think we could lift Mike that last short distance without dropping him. I looked back in desperation at Sameera, who was holding Mike's legs.

"I don't think we can do this," I called out. "Do you think we should go back?"

She shook her head. "No! We can't go back. We can do this. We're almost there."

Inch by painful inch, we gained the edge of the lip. Mike reached up above his head to clasp Jim's hand, a student who was waiting at the top to help pull him up. Despite his excruciating pain, Mike was now doing his part to help. Mac had a death grip on him and there was no way he was going to let him fall. With a burst of monumental determination and effort, we got him up and over the edge. We laid him in a safe spot, and collapsed. I've never been under such physical strain as I was during our ascent of the last few feet of that slope.

Light snow had began to fall and we hurried to carry Mike the remaining 30 feet to the tent that had been prepared for him. Once he was settled inside, it began to snow heavily and continued for the next 12 hours, shrouding the valley and mountains in a chilled, white blanket, two and a half feet thick. I hoped the weather wouldn't affect Mike's rescue. At the NOLS office, Mandeep had initiated the emergency response plan, which included contacting the United States Embassy to request their assistance in arranging a helicopter with the Indian Air Force, the only organization authorized, and equipped, to handle a challenging evacuation in the middle of the Himalayas.

Snow Camp

Once in the tent, Mike was made as comfortable as possible. Before long, after the pain medication took effect, his color returned and he became more relaxed, even joking about the situation. While all of this was going on, I was amazed at how well the students reacted and took on their various roles. They were happy to donate their personal equipment to help Mike to a point where I had to stop them because they'd need it themselves. Everyone selflessly pitched in: making hot drinks and food, running medical notes so Rajan could update Mandeep, sitting with Mike and reassuring him for hours, or helping provide first aid and building the splint. Later that night, some students even shared sleeping bags and pads because they'd donated their own to increase Mike's comfort, and several three-man tents were crammed with four or five students because Mike needed a tent of his own. Around 7 p.m., having left Mike with two friends to keep him comfortable and monitor his vital signs, I headed to my own tent. Rajan asked me to call Mandeep with an update, but I was more mentally and physically exhausted than I could ever remember being on any NOLS course, so I asked him to give me a minute.

For the first time throughout the ordeal, I stepped outside my controlled leader role. I crawled into my tent, buried my head in my sleeping bag, and cried. All the stress, physical exhaustion, fear, and anxiety streamed out of me. I cried with relief that the worst seemed to be over. Still, I couldn't stop my mind from worrying. Had I done everything I possibly could to help Mike? I was no medical doctor. Had I made any mistakes?

After a few minutes I snapped back into course leader mode and made the update call to Mandeep. He told me that the Indian Air Force had been given authority to attempt a rescue mission at first light the next morning, weather permitting. Craving some professional reassurance, I asked him if he could connect me with a doctor or medical professional who could advise me on Mike's condition and tell me how to administer short-term care of an open fracture and how to best handle his pain management. Our small supply of medication was rapidly being depleted. It was arranged that I call the Curriculum Director at the Wilderness Medicine Institute of NOLS, and author of the *NOLS Wilderness First Aid* book. He reassured me that I was doing a good job—which was a huge relief—and that I should look at the wound and evaluate Mike's foot for circulation, sensation, and movement, as well as for any signs of dead tissue. He also suggested starting Mike on an antibiotic to fight possible infection. As Mike's father, who had been informed of the accident, had requested to speak to him, we made the call and brought the phone over to Mike's tent. After speaking with his father, Mike seemed in good spirits, and I hunkered down and chatted with him for a while. Eventually he got an awkward look on his face and told me he needed to use the bathroom. Number two. *Okay*, I thought. *Well, we can do this.* I was hoping it wouldn't happen, but you know, if he's gotta go... And there was no way Mike—who was resembling a trussed-up mummy at this point—would be able to leave the tent and go on his own. It was quite the procedure to partially unwrap Mike and get him into a position to be able to take care of the matter. After several improvised methods failed, I ended up lining a cooking pot with a plastic bag and, trouper that he was, Mike made it work. I also got him to pee in a bottle so I could inspect his urine for any trace of blood. I was still concerned he might have internal injuries as a result of the bruises on his lower back. Thankfully he checked out okay and I left him to pass the night monitored by Sameera and another student, Ron.

The valley the day of the accident. *Shawn Stratton*

The valley the day after the accident. *Shawn Stratton*

The snow continued to fall heavily. Around 3 a.m., I had to clear it away from our tent while Rajan made the rounds checking on the students and waking them so they could do the same. If snow accumulated too heavily on the walls of our tents, it would block airflow in the tent. As it was an early fall expedition, we weren't fully prepared for these extreme conditions and had to resort to shoveling with frying pans and pot lids. No one got much sleep that night.

By 6:30 a.m. the cloud ceiling was very low and snow was still falling. The helicopter pilot was on standby 200 miles away at an air force base, waiting for the weather to clear. I periodically checked on Mike, who was in too much pain to get any proper rest. At one point he admitted, "I don't think I can make it through another night like this." I desperately wished I could do something. But all I could hope was that the relentless snow, the only heavy snowfall we'd encountered the entire trip, would ease up and grant our rescue helicopter safe passage through the mountains.

"Take Me to the Choppaa!"

As the cloud cover lifted and the first fingers of dawn traced the sweeps and plains of the mountains, all I could think of was getting the chopper in safely, and soon. The previous night when I'd described our location to Mandeep, I hadn't been sure a helicopter could land near our site. We were on a small ledge on the side hill of a steep valley. Mandeep had told me that the Indian Air Force helicopter was equipped with a lowering winch and, if they couldn't land, they would send down a padded strap to go under Mike's armpits and lift him up. My first thought had been: *Holy shit! A padded strap? This guy has a broken leg with a bone sticking out. Can't you do anything better than a padded strap?*

Time ticked on and the snow continued to fall. I had my eyes glued to a gadget that was reading the barometric pressure. I sent intermittent updates to Mandeep, which he relayed to the pilot who was on standby. My optimism stirred with every slight rise in pressure and, at 9:30 a.m., Mandeep called to tell us the helicopter was due to arrive around 10:30 a.m. I was surprised they were even going to leave, because the conditions were still so bad, but he assured me that the satellite image showed pockets of clear sky approaching.

The group now scrambled to move tents to clear a landing platform while I prepared Mike's splint for the flight. Knowing the consequences for Mike if the helicopter couldn't land, I was determined to make the best possible landing pad. The snow was beneficial because the tussocks were covered and we were able to make an adequate landing zone. We marked the parameters with weighted food zip bags. We also painted a large X in the middle of the landing pad with red Kool-Aid. Miraculously, by 10 a.m. the snowfall finally eased and the promised patches of blue sky began to peek out from above. It was as if we were holding one collective breath as we scrutinized the sky, anticipating the helicopter's appearance.

At last I heard an unmistakable *thump, thump, thump* and, straining my eyes, I spotted the tiny dot coming up the valley. The helicopter was flying extremely high because of the treacherous mountain terrain and unreliable weather conditions. I watched as the speck passed over our location without seeing us. As I watched it fly farther up the valley, I was getting concerned, but finally the helicopter turned around, dropping in elevation, and spotted our landing zone. At the same time we realized our tents were too close to the area and we hastily set about moving them. As the helicopter got closer, I ran to the tents while yelling at the two students who had remained by our tents to hold on to them and to watch out for the ferocious spindrift. I imagined one of the tents getting sucked up into the helicopter rotors and causing it to crash. The students held on with all their might as the helicopter descended.

The Indian Air Force rescue helicopter coming in for a landing, directly over the tents. *Connor Flanagan*

The helicopter was suddenly right above us. It hovered over the landing zone for about 30 seconds, which seemed like an eternity, like a giant humming insect, inspecting and weighing the strange environment. *LAND, GODDAMMIT, LAND!* I was saying to myself. But just as fast as it had come in, the helicopter rose and flew off.

My heart sank.

But after a few moments, it appeared as if the helicopter was turning around. Perhaps the pilot just wanted to have a closer look at the area before landing. We didn't have time to collapse the tents before the helicopter was above us again and we just had to hold on to them and bury our heads as an enormous wall of blowing snow thundered our way. The pilot powered down but left the engine and rotor running. Most helicopters don't like to fly above 9,000 feet, let alone land at 12,000 feet in challenging weather, where ice build-up on the rotors is a possibility. The dramatic landing was received with whoops and hollers of excitement. Our team was on cloud nine. One student yelled "This is so cool!" and, as uniformed men looking like paratroopers jumped out, Mike turned into Arnold Schwarzenegger from *Terminator II*, announcing in a cheery, heavily accented voice, "Take me to the choppaa!"

Within minutes he was loaded safely inside and, with another blast of snow, the helicopter left to carry him to Delhi, several hundred miles away.

The group was elated and amazed by what had taken place over the last 20 hours. People were laughing and hugging each other. For the second time in less than a day, I buried my head—in the snow this time—and wept. Then I jumped up and triumphantly rugby-tackled the first guy I saw in celebration. We'd done it. We'd pulled together and we'd pulled it off: a daring rescue in the middle of a snowstorm deep in the Himalayas.

After the Storm

Mike arrived safely at the Apollo Hospital in Delhi roughly 25 hours after his accident. He kept detailed notes throughout his hospital stay, so that when we wrapped up the Himalayan Mountains course five days later and I headed to Delhi to catch up with him, he had plenty of stories to tell—many entertaining, a few disgusting. He was meticulous about documenting, in photos, the various stages of his leg reconstruction. He told me that when the ER team removed his splint, they were amused by the random objects it encompassed. His dressings were saturated with blood, the sign of a seeping wound we hadn't detected due to the dark red fleece vest I'd used as part of the splint.

Ironically, despite the fact that Mike had reached a place of professional medical care, his first three hours at the hospital were some of his most painful. First, his wound was cleaned and bandaged. Then, when the orthopedic surgeon came to take a look, it was unwrapped and bandaged again. Another doctor came to review the leg and, once again, it was undressed and redressed, all the while without any pain medication, because apparently he'd already received the maximum he could take before surgery. Mike went in for surgery at 7:30 p.m. He underwent three more surgeries over the next two weeks in Delhi before heading back home. In New York he was admitted to the NYU Hospital for Joint Diseases, where he once more endured another battery of surgeries. In the two and half years following his accident, Mike had a total of nine surgical procedures. He still has a rod and several pins in his leg, and he deals with intermittent pain when the weather changes. Running, especially downhill, is a challenge because of the lack of muscle and ligaments, and he sports a "pretty vicious" scar, which he says he loves because it's a part of him now and it shows what he went through. Undeterred from wilderness exploration, Mike took an internship at NOLS the summer after his accident with the dream of one day becoming an instructor when his leg fully healed. As of 2013 Mike is living in New York and working for a publishing firm that creates publications for doctors continuing their medical education.

In retrospect, I see that experience as one of the best examples of real-life teamwork I've ever encountered. Every member of the group pulled together to help Mike. It was fortunate that the accident happened toward the end of the course, because by that time the group was a gelled unit, equipped with key survival skills they had learned in the course. Each member played an integral role, which is crucial for a team's success, especially in a crisis situation. If it had been just me and one student with a phone, or even me and two instructors and a phone, we wouldn't have managed such a daring rescue.

To this day, whenever I hear a helicopter I get flashbacks to Mike's rescue in the middle of a snowstorm, surrounded by towering mountains, deep within the Himalayas.

Lesson: Know Your Role

To be a high-performance team, each member should know his or her role, accept it, and take pride in their contribution. One person's role may seem mundane, like moving a tent or making soup, while someone else is responsible for something more critical, like carrying a victim or administering emergency first aid. Yet, each role is critical to the overall success of the mission. Furthermore, every role should be performed to the best ability of each person... And Then Some.

Do the members on your team know their roles?

BE CAREFUL WHAT YOU WISH FOR

Photo: Scott Silverston

CHAPTER 2

THERE ARE FEW CHALLENGES FOR A NOLS INSTRUCTOR quite like spending three full months instructing one group of students out in the wilderness. This type of semester-long assignment is called "proctoring," and generally involves 75 to 90 days of one continuous expedition, usually broken up into three or four sets of activities. Proctoring is a unique, almost overwhelming, experience. It's especially fulfilling for someone who thrives on building teams. You get to watch your students grow in ways you couldn't observe on a shorter course. We all know each other inside out. Spending just seven days with someone in the wilderness is like getting to know someone in the "ordinary" world for a year. This experience can be awesome; or just as easily, a nightmare. When you think about what it would be like to spend that much time, day and night, with, say, your work colleagues, or anyone you know, cooking together, eating together, sleeping beside each other, you can imagine how it might get challenging. Which is probably why some of the strangest experiences and encounters I've ever had occured while I was proctoring.

The other challenging aspect from an instructor's point of view is that it's also exhausting, certainly from a physical perspective, but even more so mentally. As an instructor, you always have to be *on*. You're not going to kick back and have a beer; you're constantly thinking about where everyone is and if they're safe. An instructor is role-modeling 24/7 and the students are watching to see what you're doing. If you swear, if you're lazy, if you don't cook good meals, if you snap or seem to be in a bad mood—they'll pick up that too.

I'd been eager to begin proctoring ever since joining NOLS, and my first experience took me to the Alaskan Arctic. I was the sole instructor chosen to stay and mentor a group of 12 students for all three sections of a semester. The first month we backpacked, the second we sea kayaked, and the third took us river canoeing. At the start of each section, a fresh instructor specializing in that particular activity joined the group. In Alaska, by the time we entered the third section, I was starting to feel the toll of proctoring. The first two sections, backpacking and sea kayaking, had gone well. We experienced the usual troubles and delays from bad weather, minor injuries, and group dynamics, but nothing out of the ordinary. So I wasn't worried about the last section: 18 days of Arctic river canoeing. I was expecting it to be the easiest and most straightforward of the three. We could carry more supplies, thanks to our canoes, and the river we were scheduled to travel down looked tame.

In fact, Kent, my new co-instructor for this section, was worried it was too tame. Always confident and adventurous, Kent was a skilled, experienced paddler, and I was glad to have him along for the rest of the course. We had met at the beginning of the section at the NOLS Alaska branch in Palmer. We were there with the group for two days to switch our gear and re-stock our supplies after our sea kayaking trip. After we'd had a chance to catch up and he'd met the team, Kent admitted he wasn't too excited about the route we were scheduled to take.

"I don't know, Shawn," he said. "I think we're really going to have to sell this river to keep the group interested."

I looked at him through a haze of disguised exhaustion (in contrast to Kent's own fresh-instructor energy), but nonetheless couldn't help but agree after examining the maps and learning more about our route. Despite the fact that I was drained, I didn't find the next section of the course compelling either. For the next 18 days we were supposed to paddle Beaver Creek and the Yukon River, starting 100 miles north of Fairbanks in the White Mountains. The route had never been paddled by a NOLS group before and only half of it had been scouted by NOLS staff the previous year. According to reports and maps, the river appeared flat and unexciting compared to some of the white-water rivers that NOLS paddles in the area. Maybe I needed something more dynamic to boost my enthusiasm and energy. Little did I know at that point quite how dynamic—or rather, dramatic—things were about to get.

The slow and meandering Beaver Creek, Alaska. *Kathryn Atkinson*

Kent and I reviewed the maps. The river started in the White Mountains, where we would experience a little white-water action while cruising through the beautiful rolling mountains. This all sounded good, but after six days we'd enter the Yukon Flats National Wildlife Refuge, which on the map appeared to be a 500-square-mile bog. We would then paddle through this quiet water for about two weeks before floating out the Yukon River, the third largest river in North America. The idea of spending two weeks essentially bog paddling had us disheartened. Staring down at the tranquil course outlined on the map, Kent and I immediately searched for alternate routes to liven things up. We decided to stretch out the initial section in the White Mountains as long as we could by having several layover days, giving us time for hiking and fishing. We soon learned, however, that sometimes the adventure comes to you.

Mysterious Missile

On our second day's hike, in between paddling the shallows of Beaver Creek, the first in a string of strange events happened. The group had set a goal to climb to the top of a nearby mountain. We wanted to glimpse the terrain we'd be encountering over the days to come. We hiked up the scree field ridge, an accumulation of broken rock fragments skirting the barren mountain. The warm, dry, August air carried a woodsy scent from the drifting smoke of far-off forest fires. As we scanned the hazy, blue-green horizon, one of the students pointed to something shimmering among the rocks, just a few hundred yards away. We speculated that it was a survey marker for a boundary or a mine and decided to check it out on the way down. After spending time on the summit, where we ate lunch and took photos of a nearby caribou, a few of us hiked off to investigate the shiny object. In high spirits, the students ran ahead. When I arrived, they were gathered around a large silver cylinder.

It was a missile.

Holy crap.

The missile was at least 10 feet high, sticking up out of the ground, with its tip buried and its wings protruding at the top. The students turned to me, their eyes wide.

"Er... we all agreed not to touch it," said Mel, one of the girls. "We're worried it might blow up."

Students check out the missile. *Heath Milligan*

I was perplexed. "What's a missile doing all the way out here?" Our location was remote, for sure, but usually military testing occurs in secure, designated areas.

I walked over and thoroughly examined it, but all I could find was a serial number. And then, probably for badness as much as anything else, I tapped it a few times. The group gasped. "Relax," I laughed. "If it didn't go off slamming into the ground, I think we're pretty safe."

But it was weird. I could only imagine how we'd have reacted if it had landed while we were in the area. Part of me wondered whether we should contact the authorities. After taking a few photos, we left the mysterious missile, joined the others, and headed back to camp. On the way we had fun making up stories to explain why it was there. *Was it Russian? Was there a special top-secret James-Bond-style lair nestled in the mountains?* It was just the sort of area in which you might expect to find one.

Tooth and Claw

Happy with our mountain hike and our mysterious missile encounter, we headed down the peak in the sunshine, strolling through glowing Arctic tundra and picking fat blueberries. As our camp along the river below came into view, someone pointed out that a tent was missing. We were still fairly far away, so we thought it must be behind one of the other tents, hidden from view. But as we hiked closer, the tent was still nowhere to be seen. The only thing I could think of was that high winds had blown it down the gravel bar or into the river. But this scenario didn't fit.

My suspicions were confirmed. The area was a disaster. All our tents and most of our gear had been ransacked and shredded. The missing tent was right where we'd pitched it but now lying flat with two snapped poles sticking out of the tattered nylon. The other four tents all had one broken pole each and numerous rips from what appeared to be the claws of a large beast. The only explanation: a bear. Several sleeping bags and pads had also been dragged out into the open and shredded along with several dry bags, and even a rubber boot bore puncture wounds rendered by large pointy teeth. We all stared, mouths agape in shock. A few beats of silence, then suddenly everyone seemed to fly off the handle at once. A few of the students were in tears. They wanted to rush in and assess the violation to their personal belongings, but my first reaction was to hold still. "Stop. Don't touch anything. We need to take photos," I said.

Tents mauled by the bear. *Kathryn Atkinson*

The destruction was so shocking I wanted to document it. I knew we might need to get emergency supplies flown in and that would cost NOLS a fortune. I felt that no one would quite believe the extent of the mutilation without some proof. I also didn't want the students in their agitation to make any of the damage worse. We needed to evaluate the situation and form a plan; we needed to see if we could make repairs. My next concern was for our food supply. My heart lurched. I grabbed two students and we sprinted downstream to where we kept our food neatly tucked away in large dry bags on the ground. When camping in bear country we typically set up camp in a triangle, with tents, kitchen, and food storage at each point. We try not to leave any "smellies," including sunscreen or toothpaste, around our tents and avoid putting candy wrappers in our pockets, as bears are attracted to them. We aim to keep our kitchens downwind from the tents and extremely tidy and free of any food scraps. We either suspend our food from trees or, in the Arctic, where the trees are not tall enough, we store them in barrels or dry bags 300 feet from the kitchen. To my surprise, and relief, the bags were untouched, and there was no sign of bear activity near them. Now I *really* was confused.

Rushing about camp, surveying the damage and taking inventory, we noticed that the animal seemed to have clawed into the tents through the windows in the roofs and vestibules. Sleeping bags were partially hanging out of the windows of a few tents. It was as if the bear had used each tent as a trampoline, launching itself, claws and teeth first, from one to the next. Despite years of experience traveling in bear country, I couldn't explain or understand this behavior at all. To this day, I've never seen or heard anything quite like it. Why in the world would a bear destroy our tents like this and not touch our food? Once we surveyed the damage and recovered from our shock, we shifted into repair mode. I was still thinking we'd probably have to call our base to get new tents and other gear airdropped in, but I knew the gravel bar we were on wasn't big enough to allow even a small bush plane to land. Kent and I pondered our options and we agreed to try to repair the tents before considering requesting a difficult and costly airdrop.

To begin, we dismantled the tents and separated them into tent bodies, flies, and poles. We gathered the damaged personal equipment. Luckily, we'd assembled an extensive repair kit for the expedition, which gave us a fighting chance. We split the team into four groups, each with a specific task. Several students repaired personal equipment (sleeping bags, sleeping pads, rubber boots, and dry bags), and the rest the tent bodies, flies, and poles. In our new reality, duct tape and seam seal became the most valuable items in our possession as we patched up jagged tears in tent nylon and used a small hack saw to make splints to repair broken poles. At one point, we spotted what we could only assume was the guilty culprit: a black bear, strolling nonchalantly across the gravel bar several hundred yards away. Worried that he might be coming back for another attack, we told the group to be prepared to pack up and move downstream if he started hanging around.

Throughout the evening and into the night we worked tirelessly to resurrect each tent. By 10 p.m., we were satisfied with the jobs done and thought about going to bed. The tents were covered in seam-seal glue and would need to dry overnight before we could use them. That meant that we would need to crash out under the stars. I usually enjoy sleeping outside, but northern Alaska is a land where mosquitos resemble small birds and they were out that night in full force. We set up tarps to shelter us in case it rained, but by 2 a.m. the mosquitos were so voracious that some students got up to build a fire in the hope that the smoke would deter them—and any more marauding bears, for that matter. Fortunately the repairs held up and we continued using the now disheveled looking tents for the remainder of the trip.

The culprit black bear. *Neuvi Villanueva*

Arctic Circle Diversion

A few days later, our flotilla paddled out of the White Mountains, continued down Beaver Creek, and stroke by stroke entered the Yukon Flats National Wildlife Refuge, 6.5 million acres of mostly flat and undulating lowlands.

Beaver Creek by this time in the dry season had turned into a slow-moving stream. For a group of young adventurers eager for a fast river with occasional rapids, the creek was a disappointment, just as Kent and I had feared. As the land around us was flat and unchanging, we had no points of reference or landmarks. Usually on a river, you can at least follow the topography of the shoreline, but after 30 or 40 almost identical S bends, we'd lost count, along with a sense of exactly where we were.

Beaver Creek in the Yukon Flats National Wildlife Refuge. *Kathryn Atkinson*

When Kent and I had studied our route before the trip, we noticed that another creek, Birch Creek, flowed within a mile of Beaver Creek at one point and also emptied into the Yukon River. The appeal of Birch Creek was it would only take three days to reach the Yukon, instead of the seven days Beaver Creek would take. In addition, Birch Creek emptied into the Yukon approximately 10 miles downstream from where a bend crossed the Arctic Circle, offering us a chance to reach the landmark, an exciting bonus.

After a few days of boring canoeing and tedious navigation, and after much debate and trepidation, Kent and I hatched a plan. We decided to present the group with the option to go rogue for the next seven days. Before presenting our case, we explained that there was a strong possibility it might not work out and so everyone had to agree with the change of plans. Our idea was to portage (carry) our canoes and gear overland one mile from Beaver Creek to Birch Creek and then paddle three days down to meet the Yukon River. There, we'd attempt to paddle 10 miles upstream over two days and officially cross the Arctic Circle.

"Before you make a decision," I told the group, "we have to let you know the potential problems."

They waited while I spread out the map and pointed to the rivers.

"First, we have to figure out exactly where we are, because the creeks flow a mile apart for only a short section, then they veer off in different directions. If we miss that mile-long section, we'll have a problem, because there's no way we want to carry our gear for more than a mile."

I paused.

"Even a mile will be tough," explained Kent.

"Exactly. Also, that one mile has to be walkable, and with so much bog and thick brush around, it might turn out to be the hardest part of the whole mission."

"And the water levels need to be high enough to paddle the canoes," said Kent. "There's no way of knowing if they will be. Once we get to the Yukon River, the flow and terrain will have to be just right for us to paddle upstream for 10 miles."

"If any of these four obstacles proves too difficult, we'll have no chance of touching the Arctic Circle," I concluded.

The students looked from the map to each other and back to the map. We were on day 67 of 74 and everyone was a little worn down. I didn't think the group would go for the proposed adventure. To my surprise, however, all but one student supported the plan. Those in favor quickly convinced that person. The group was as ready for a challenge as we were.

Kent and I met with the student Leaders of the Day, spread out our maps, and fine-tuned our plan. If we were where we thought we were, reaching the section where a portage would be possible could happen tomorrow. Each Leader of the Day has an increase in responsibilities and takes turns leading peers for a day. It provides opportunities for students to practice leadership roles.

As we paddled the next day, we all watched our maps like hawks, making sure not to float by our intended campsite and portage-launching point. We got to camp in the early afternoon and set out to scout a walkable route to Birch Creek. Everyone was excited to see if the navigation was accurate and Birch Creek was really only a mile away. As we had anticipated, the terrain was dotted with bogs, dense shrubs, and thick stands of boreal forest. After 45 minutes scouting the area, we came across Birch Creek, and it appeared to have plenty of water to carry us down to the Yukon River. The portage would be a challenge but doable.

The following day we prepared the equipment as best we could for carrying. Unlike many canoe trips with planned portages where people are prepared for a hike with their equipment, we fell woefully short. It took us the entire day and several trips to make the move to Birch Creek. At times the forest was so thick we were pushing the canoes on our heads through the trees and, when we took a break, the canoe just stayed, jammed up in the foliage. But in the end, with our gear moved and mission accomplished, we were elated to have already successfully tackled three of our four potential deal-breaking obstacles.

Portaging through dense forest. *Neuvi Villanueva*

Over the next two and a half days we paddled easily down Birch Creek until we hit the Yukon River. As we approached the junction where the creek dumped into the giant expanse, we noticed the water changing color from clear to the recognizable murky grey of the Yukon, caused by glacial silt. Our excitement grew as we studied the river. How strong would the current be? Would there be any chance of paddling upstream?

As our canoes nudged into the Yukon, we pointed our bows upstream and paddled harder than we ever had. We made progress, inch by inch. The undulating shore of the giant river allowed us to "eddy hop" our way upstream several hundred yards. An eddy is a place in a river where the water moves in a different direction or different speed than the main current, thanks to rocks, outcroppings, logs, bridge pilings, or the inside bends of a river. When we got to a point in the river where there were no eddies and the current was too strong to paddle upstream, we got out of our canoes and dragged them, walking along the shoreline. These two methods combined worked quite well. By nightfall, we had moved half the distance upriver to the Arctic Circle.

The calm before the storm, drifting down the expansive Yukon River. *Kathryn Atkinson*

The following morning started as usual with a route briefing from the designated Leader of the Day. If everything went as planned, we could reach our final destination before nightfall. Everyone was invigorated about the opportunity to cross the Arctic Circle. After just five hours of paddling, dragging, and ferrying our canoes upstream, we determined, using the surrounding topography, that we had indeed crossed the Arctic Circle. We were 66° 33' 39" north of the equator! We pulled the canoes over to the riverbank and had a group hug.

Then we jumped into the frigid Yukon River to celebrate.

Gone with the Wind

The final section of our expedition involved canoeing the Yukon River for five days until we reached our pick-up destination, where the river crosses the Dalton Highway, one of the most isolated roads in the United States. The end of our three-month expedition was in sight. For three of the final five days, the students would travel in two groups (boys and girls separately) without instructors on a small-group expedition. These mini-excursions usually last from three to 10 days, depending on location, the group's abilities, and the course schedule. They are opportunities for students to use their own judgment and practice the outdoor teamwork and risk management skills they've already learned, free from instructors, who can be up to 24 hours away at any given time. Participating in a small-group expedition is often the highlight of an entire course: an earned reward.

Course instructors decide if each student is ready to take part in the student-led expedition. In most cases all students participate. By this time, they've already learned basic wilderness first aid and, before the groups set out, we go over detailed emergency procedures and make sure everyone is aware of the other group's campsites by marking them on maps. We made camp at the Arctic Circle to review the route and emergency procedures. The plan was for the students to leave first and get to their respective camps before us. The instructor's camp would be located farther down the river. The two student groups set off ahead, but, before long, Kent and I caught up with them, so we eventually passed by and moved ahead out of the way.

Shawn with a student scouting the Yukon River. *Neuvi Villanueva*

In the early afternoon of the first day, we paddled by the remote Native American community of Beaver, noting there was surprisingly little activity on the shoreline. As if on cue, the wind, already quite blustery, suddenly picked up, and strengthened throughout the day. By evening it was gusting so powerfully in our faces that Kent and I struggled to paddle against it, barely making progress.

The gale reached a point that further paddling would be dangerous, so we pulled off the river to make camp. We hoped the student groups had decided to do the same. The Yukon River is more than half a mile wide in sections and very different from the small creeks we'd been paddling for most of the expedition. As a group, we'd not experienced wind like this and I was concerned for the students. We set up camp, battling the gusting wind, which tore at our gear and threatened to fling it into the wilderness. Once we had everything secured, we settled down to watch for the two groups in case they paddled by. We hoped to pull them over and cancel the small-group expedition. No one appeared and eventually Kent and I went to bed, as howling gusts of wind battered our tent seams.

We woke in the morning to the steady flap, flap, flap of the wind still beating against our already weakened tent like a loose tarp covering a mattress on the roof of a car. The weather hadn't relented through the night; to our shock, it had intensified. We poked our heads outside to see two-foot waves rolling and blowing upstream. There was still no sign of the students. With the terrible paddling conditions, we hoped they'd gotten off the river the day before and were hunkered down, waiting for the wind to relent. Knowing that they had never seen conditions like this before, we weren't sure how they would react. We hoped that the wilderness-savvy judgment we had cultivated over the semester would now kick in.

Kent and I spent most of the day cooped up in the tent discussing the semester and writing student evaluations, a dreaded paperwork-heavy task that comes at the end of every NOLS course. We poked our heads out the tent door occasionally to look for any students that might be floating by and to check the river conditions. The wind was so strong that the gritty silt from the gravel bar we were camped on pierced through the zippers and seams of the tent, covering everything with a fine grey coating. Evening came and went with no sign of the students and no reprieve from the weather. We hoped that they had slipped by us and were waiting for us at our predetermined campsite.

The next morning we packed up camp and pressed forward to the campsite where we planned to meet the students, in case they were already there. The wind raged so powerfully that it blew our loaded canoe upstream in the opposite direction many times. We paddled close to shore and, after several hours of inching along, had to give up. We decided to pull off, have a snack, and reassess our plan. As we discussed our options, we looked across the river and spotted a small group of people. We were excited, thinking it was the guys' group. Kent and I jumped back into our canoe and set off to meet them. Because the angle of our canoe was now parallel to the waves, the water crashed over its side. Nearly halfway across, I realized with a jolt that in our haste we hadn't tied down all our equipment as we usually do. With water now slurping inside our canoe, it was becoming increasingly unstable. If we flipped now, we risked losing everything, including the first-aid kit and satellite phone. With no choice but to put our heads down and power through, we paddled furiously. Sweat blew sideways off our foreheads as we cranked on our paddles, our chests about to explode with exertion and fear. It was the most terrifying time I've ever spent in a fully loaded canoe.

To make things worse, as we neared the opposite shore we realized this wasn't the boys' group but a random group of paddlers trying to navigate their way down the angry river. They were German tourists and, except for their guide, appeared to be novices. They'd also pulled off the river because of the dangerous conditions. Their guide, deciding it would be best for them to construct a catamaran with their canoes to make them more stable, was chopping down trees. One of the tourists was near hysteria. She told us they were inexperienced paddlers and she didn't think they should be on the water in these conditions.

"What are *you* doing out here?" she asked us.

Kent and I looked at each other. "We're guides," I said, not wanting to get into the spiel of what it means to be a wilderness leadership instructor.

"Well, where's your group?"

"Good question." I explained we weren't really sure. It didn't feel good saying the words out loud, and the sound of the vast rushing river behind me only intensified my fears. "But don't worry," I added. "Our students are fully equipped and have been living in the Alaskan wilderness for almost three months. They know how to handle themselves."

Kent gave me a look and I could tell he was thinking the same thing: *We hope.*

After the tourists had constructed their catamarans, they paddled off, wobbling into the wind. Kent and I watched, doubtful the logs would stay tied to the canoes for long, but we were intrigued by the idea.

We hunkered down to review the maps and do a few calculations regarding our progress. With our current location, weather conditions, and the fact that we didn't know where our students were, we were worried we wouldn't make our pick-up at the Dalton Highway. We still had a few days, but we thought we should contact the NOLS Alaska branch office to let them know our situation. This was a phone call we didn't want to make but we knew it would be appreciated at the branch so they could organize potential rescue plans. When you're an expedition leader, calling your supervisor and letting him know you're winded in and may not reach your pick-up is one thing; but, not only were we winded in, we also had no idea where our students were.

The leaders back at the branch weren't too concerned when we spoke to them, given we still had three days to reach our final destination if the wind relented. They thanked us for the call and asked us to ring back in 24 hours with an update.

Having been off the river for over an hour, we decided to get back in our canoe and keep forging ahead. Within a few hours, we saw the hapless German group on the side of the river again, but this time it looked as if they were setting up camp for the night. They hadn't made much progress with the catamaran. Kent and I pushed on for another hour until we reached the camp location where we were supposed to meet the students. Exhausted and disappointed not to see anyone else there, we hauled the canoe onto the gravel bar and set up camp again in the face of a howling gale.

The next morning we called the branch with an update straight away. We knew that because we hadn't seen the students by now, there was a very good chance we wouldn't make it to the pick-up on time. Our contact told us they'd heard from Will, the boys' group leader: everyone in their group was safe and they'd been camping in the tiny village of Beaver since the first day of the small-group expedition. Fortunately, they'd pulled off the water early on, as soon as the winds started to pick up. Kent and I were delighted. The girls' group wasn't with them, however, and Will didn't know where they were. The guys told the branch they thought the girls might be camped upstream not far off. The branch told Will to keep his group where they were and await further instruction.

At daybreak the next day, still completely winded in, Kent and I again called the branch. And once again, our contact had news: the previous day the wind had died down enough near Beaver that the locals felt confident taking their motorboats out. One of the locals offered to take Will upstream to look for the girls' group, which they discovered not too far along the river. The girls had draped clothing, equipment, and gear along the shore, in line with their emergency procedures training, to alert anyone passing by that they were there and needed help. Once they were reunited, Will explained the situation and told them now that the wind had subsided, they should paddle downstream to Beaver where they could join the guys and wait for further instruction.

Kent and I were thrilled to learn both our groups were safe and reunited. We spent the rest of the blustery day finishing our evaluations and brainstorming ways to get off the river in time to end the course on schedule. The students had flights to catch right after the course and I was supposed to be best man at a wedding in Newfoundland (five and a half time zones and 5,000 miles away) two days after the course ended. With the ever-persistent wind, we all risked missing our flights.

Back at the branch, our colleagues had also been brainstorming different scenarios to get our team and seven canoes off the river. After talking several times with our contact on the satellite phone, a plan was devised. NOLS decided that the best way to get to the students would be to charter a plane to Beaver and fly them to Fairbanks to be picked up in the bus. Since the chartered planes would fly in empty, and the canoes needed to be transported, they asked several instructors who happened to be at the branch if they wanted to do a free fly-in canoe trip. Most of the instructors had just finished their own Alaska courses and were just hanging out at the branch. The mission would be to drop the instructors off so they could paddle the canoes back down the river to the Dalton Highway for pick-up. There they would be met with the van and canoe trailer. Nine instructors volunteered, thrilled at the chance for a fun, free expedition.

Head-to-toe dress for the legendary Alaskan mosquitos at camp on the Yukon River. *Scott Silverston*

We now had a plan to get the students and canoes off the river, which just left me and Kent and, of course, our equipment. We had a thorough look at the gravel bar where we were camped. I was sure a small bush plane could land and pick us up, but the problem would be getting the canoe. The Branch Director didn't want us to stash the canoe out in the woods in the middle of the

Yukon River. That left us with one option: to paddle on as we'd originally intended. The problem was, we were scheduled to be picked up at 11 a.m. the next day and there was still a long way left to go. The only chance of making the pick-up on time was if the wind dropped, if we paddled like crazy for most of the night and got up very early the next morning.

Sunset after the storm on the Yukon River. *Shawn Stratton*

By 6 p.m. the tenacious wind finally eased. We figured this would be our only opportunity to get off the river in time to meet our pick-up and get me to the wedding in Newfoundland. We took advantage of the late-August Alaskan twilight to navigate our way. Around 1 a.m., with darkness imminent, we narrowly missed hitting a tree stump stuck in the river that surely would have thrown us into the water, so we decided it was time to catch a few hours sleep.

At 4:30 a.m. our alarms went off. We needed to get back on the river if we had any hope of reaching our pick-up on time. After several hours of paddling, we calculated our rate of travel and were excited to realize that we could make the pick-up on schedule at 11 a.m. I'll never forget calling the branch on the satellite phone as I sat, arms aching, in the bow of the canoe in the middle of the Yukon River with the news that we were going to make it on time.

We pulled up to the boat ramp underneath the Dalton Highway Bridge that spans the Yukon River at 10:55 a.m. I was so excited to finally be off the river, knowing I'd catch my flight. I ran up to the parking lot to look for the NOLS van, but it wasn't there. We unloaded all our gear, pulled up the canoe and waited. As one hour slipped by, and then another, and another, our frustration mounted. We were exhausted and it had taken all the energy we had to get to the bridge on time. Our ride showed up at 4 p.m. The driver hadn't received word we would make it to the bridge by 11 a.m. and had been in Fairbanks shopping with his girlfriend.

By this time I was at the end of my rope. Heading back to Fairbanks where we would stay before being reunited with our students the next day, I told Kent there was no way I was spending one more night camping.

"I'm splurging on a hotel room. I've spent 74 days leading the longest expedition of my life and all I want is a shower and a real bed."

"Amen," said Kent.

It's Not Over Till You're Back at the Branch

On arriving that evening, we discovered that Jim, the NOLS Alaska Branch Director, had already booked us a room at a nice Fairbanks hotel. After checking in, we tossed our spare set of clothes in the washer and practically sprinted over to the "most northern Denny's in the world," which happened to be next door. It seemed to take forever to be served, but that was probably because we still hadn't showered and were wearing the same clothes for the better part of a month. Eventually our food arrived and we inhaled it. During dinner, we talked about how surreal it was that we were eating at Denny's in Fairbanks and our students, our responsibility, were 500 miles away camping on the Yukon River. We probably set a NOLS record that night for being the farthest distance away from our students while a course was still in progress.

The next morning we met up with the instructors at the airport as they waited to board the plane that would drop them off for their impromptu canoe expedition and pick up our stranded group. The plane had empty seats, so Kent and I hopped in for the flight. It was fascinating to fly over the area we'd spent the last three weeks paddling.

When we arrived in Beaver, all the students were at the runway to greet us. It was like a mini-reunion; we were originally supposed to be apart for just two and half days but it had now been seven. We quickly loaded their gear on the plane, said goodbye to the other instructors, and flew back to Fairbanks. During the flight and the bus ride back to the branch, everyone shared stories about their experiences.

Will told us that his motorboat mission to look for the girls had been diverted into a mildly disturbing impromptu hunting trip thanks to the shotgun-happy boat owner. They'd spotted and chased a grizzly bear along the way and then the boat owner had cornered a moose on a gravel bar. "The guy was trying to aim the gun, steer the boat, and battle the wind at the same time," said Will. "He was swerving all over the place. Eventually I had to literally hit the deck to avoid being shot. He took the animal down, but when we went over to look, it was still alive, convulsing and bleeding all over the place. So he shot it one more time—at close range—and said, 'Would you like to stay and help me clean him?' I think by this time I was in a state of shock and I just said, 'I'd really like to find my friends if that's okay.' You can imagine I was pretty happy when we finally spotted the girls' camp."

The girls were happy too. Unlike the guys, who had been passing the time in a small community, enjoying village life, and talking with the branch, they'd been stranded for three days alone on the side of a riverbank wondering what to do. They were constantly checking the weather and trying to decide if they should paddle on or stay where they were. They practiced all the leadership, teamwork, and outdoor skills they'd gained over the semester to keep them as comfortable as possible during the ordeal.

In Beaver, the guys' group had camped out in the backyard of a missionary's home, and, in addition to Will's hunting story, each member had an interesting experience to share: from teaching in the local school, to playing video games in a child's home, riding out to a cabin on an ATV, and enjoying an elaborate salmon feast.

"Oh, by the way," said Will. "Remember that missile we found a few weeks back? One of the locals told me there's a military missile-testing site in the area. Apparently they fire test shots fairly often."

"No kidding!" I shook my head. "Well that solves that mystery."

"Do they also conduct weird tests on the local bear population?" said Kent. "That would solve another."

As we headed back to the branch where we'd wrap up the course, I tried to think of the best way to sum up the extraordinary 74-day wilderness experience. One of the most important aspects of a NOLS course is taking the skills the students learn in the field and relating them to how they can be used in everyday life at home. We call making this connection "transference." I'd spent considerable time over the semester planning how I'd present transference learning to the students at the end of the course. Before the wind had foiled our expedition, we'd planned to use the last two days out in the field to take the group through several exercises. Now, instead of two days, we had just two hours, but I realized the last seven days' events had taught them far more than any contrived exercise I could have planned.

One of my favorite sayings sums up this expedition perfectly: "Don't let the education get in the way of the learning."

Silver Lining

Talk about an epic, exhausting, and eventful trip. I was so proud of our group and how they'd handled the adverse situations that confronted them, from the bear attacking our camp to the change of route and then being stranded by weather. Their experience over the seven days could never have been planned. Having tolerance during adversity and finding the ability to adapt and overcome is the essence of adventure learning and what NOLS is all about. As a leader, an excellent way to build confidence is to encourage your team members to use their judgment to make decisions with real consequences. If you guide them through all decision-making processes or tend to interject when things get difficult, they'll never learn to trust themselves. The independent student-group travel experience that happens on many outdoor education courses is an ideal way to practice this.

In the end, I made all my flight connections and, after 15 hours of travel, stood in a tux as best man at my friend's wedding in Newfoundland. It was quite the transformation to go from living in the wilderness with the same 14 people for 74 days, only having two showers and one wash of clothes, to being in church, dressed to the nines. My head was in such a fog, however, that I forgot to bring the rings—only my most important job as best man!

As the ceremony started and I realized my colossal mistake, I hastily mouthed this information to the groom, sweat beading my forehead as I envisioned the ceremony grinding to a halt while someone looked for the rings.

The groom was prepared. He had the rings in his pocket and, when everyone's heads were bowed in prayer, he slipped them to me.

Phew. Another crisis averted.

Lesson: Use Judgment

The legendary educator, mountaineer, and founder of NOLS, Paul Petzoldt, used to say to his students, "rules are for fools, use your head." When creating and developing a team it's important to establish common goals and shared values, but very few rigid rules should come into play. Guidelines can be helpful, of course, but good judgment based on common values and understanding is essential. Especially when unique circumstances appear, which they inevitably will just as likely inside an office as out in the wilderness.

How can you encourage good judgment when it comes to decision-making?

$30,000 BLISTER

Photo: Shawn Stratton

CHAPTER 3

BLISTERS. THOSE COMMON, SEEMINGLY INNOCUOUS little pressure points can be a hiker's archenemy.

I once had a student on a course in Mexico who developed six big blisters on each foot. Every new day brought a fresh bubble of pain, and we eventually had to evacuate him from the course because it became too excruciating for him to walk. Just to get him out of the mountains we had to put his swollen feet in a spare pair of camp shoes belonging to another student, who was a size 14 to his 10. They looked like clown boots. Perhaps even more excruciating for him than the physical discomfort was forfeiting an adventure that had cost thousands of dollars. All because he was wearing the wrong footwear: his father's hiking boots.

As a wilderness leader, I have a healthy respect for blisters. They're a common occurrence, but I usually pride myself on being able to treat students' blisters in the field before they get out of hand. At the beginning of every expedition instructors teach a class on blister prevention and care: how to properly tie hiking boots and how to recognize hot spots, which occur when you feel friction between your sock and boot before anything appears. Duct tape or moleskin over the area usually stops the problem. But sometimes students try to be brave and soldier on even when they feel hot spots because they don't want to make everyone stop mid-hike for them to check their feet.

Sometimes during an expedition things go on behind the scenes that I don't know about and therefore can't anticipate becoming a problem, like the student in Mexico who was wearing borrowed boots that didn't fit properly. And sometimes these factors cause a situation to escalate in unexpected and potentially dangerous ways.

I was leading a 30-day NOLS wilderness backpacking expedition in the Ogilvie Mountains, 100 miles south of the Arctic Circle in Canada's Yukon Territory. The mountain range encompasses the staggeringly beautiful Tombstone Territorial Park and is intersected by the desolate Dempster Highway, which connects Dawson City to the Arctic Ocean. To say this area is remote is an understatement. I was the course leader and Frank and Linda were my assistant instructors. The group was made up of a dozen 16- to 20-year-old students from all over the United States.

The course had been going well; we had encountered all the splendor and challenge of the majestic and imposing Ogilvie Mountains. We had traveled over vast undulating terrain, down steep mountain passes, through thick bushes, and across challenging rivers. The Yukon is an untouched wilderness paradise where few human feet ever tread. Over an entire expedition it would be unusual to bump into another person other than your fellow course mates. You're much more likely to see bears, wolves, moose, or caribou.

The Ogilvie Mountains. *Shawn Stratton*

It may have been August, but the weather consistently changed from very hot to very cold and wet to dry with a few days of snow thrown in for good measure. Some days it would be 77 degrees with the sun shining and we'd pick berries, and fish. Then the next morning we'd wake up to a layer of snow. Other days there'd be driving rain. We used to say, "Hot cold, hot cold, wet dry, wet dry. Welcome to the Yukon."

Dense mountain fog made navigation challenging. *Shawn Stratton*

With changeable, often wet weather, healthy and dry feet at the end of the day are particularly important. But a few students on this trip were dealing with some blisters, including Jen, who had a few small ones around her toes, which she treated with tape and moleskin. At 18, Jen was one of the older students on the course and a natural leader. A keen outdoors woman, she was athletic and fit. She was one of the fastest hikers in the group and was becoming more confident with her off-trail navigation. Her blisters didn't seem to give her much trouble, and she managed them well on her own.

During the middle section of the course, Jen began experiencing intermittent back pain after long days of hiking. She was a slight girl, not a big eater, and she followed a vegan diet, which meant she had brought supplemental food to offset the regular NOLS diet. To alleviate her pain she took ibuprofen and on several occasions we reduced the weight in her backpack by distributing it to others in the group. We also took the occasional rest day to give everyone time to recharge and enjoy the pristine beauty of our surroundings.

During one of our camp stops, Jen called me over to examine her feet, because she'd noticed increased redness and localized pain around some of her blisters. I could see that one of the blisters was showing signs of infection.

"Be sure to clean your feet and soak the infected area in warm water every day," I told her. "Keep a close eye on the blisters and if anything changes, let me know, especially if the pain increases."

For several days I checked in with Jen and she never complained of her blisters getting any worse. I assumed she had been cleaning and soaking them and that all was well.

We were now approaching the end of the course and everyone was preparing to head out on their small-group section. The students' Ogilvie Mountains small-group expedition was to take place over four nights and five days and end at the final campsite before our pick-up on the Dempster Highway. This was a fairly long student-led expedition for the age group and location, but we'd been impressed with the students during the course.

The day before the students left on their mini-expedition, we divided the groups, allocated food supplies, and devised routes.

Each group would hike a different route to get to the final destination campsite. Frank, Linda, and I had another look at Jen's infected toe and asked her how she felt. The toe looked better; she said she felt okay and was excited about the instructorless excursion.

Students hike through the rugged Tombstone Range of the Ogilvie Mountains. *Shawn Stratton*

Small Blister, Big Consequences

Three days later and three days into the small-group excursion, Linda, Frank, and I were already settled at the destination campsite. We were on schedule and psyching ourselves up to tackle the looming paperwork of student assessments. Around

8 p.m., we were discussing the evaluations when we heard what sounded like shouting coming from up the valley. We immediately thought it must be one of our student groups because in this remote landscape we hadn't seen another human being for the last 25 days except the helicopter pilot who delivered our rations. As the noise moved closer, we realized it was the unmistakable sound of NOLS students making bear calls: "Heyyyy bear! Heyyyy bear!" When traveling in grizzly bear territory it's important to avoid surprising these animals at close range, so we teach students to make their presence known, particularly when the terrain or vegetation makes it difficult to see.

We jumped to our feet to meet the students. My heart was pounding. I knew something was wrong. We weren't due to see the students for two more days. The only reason for them to come and find us ahead of time would be an emergency. I feared someone was seriously injured or, even worse, killed. My mind raced as I wondered who it could be and what could possibly have happened.

When we finally saw the students, the first thing I noticed was there were only two: Marlene and John. This set off more alarm bells. We were in grizzly bear territory and the students knew to always travel in groups of four people, and no fewer than three. The small groups were made up of five students. In the event a student was injured, the others were instructed to leave someone behind with the patient and send the other three to find the instructors.

Although I was extremely concerned, I tried to sound calm when I greeted them. "Hey guys, what's up?"

They were out of breath and looked a little frantic. "It's Jen's toe; she's in a lot of pain."

I let out a huge exhale.

Back at our camp, Marlene and John caught their breath and drank some water as they updated us on Jen. The previous night and that morning, Jen had complained about her toe, saying it was throbbing with pain and had kept her up most of the night. She had covered it with tape during the following day's hike and hadn't complained any further. The other students noticed, however, that toward the end of the hike she had drifted into the middle of the group, instead of leading at the front. She became very quiet and was determined to reach camp quickly. At camp she told Janet, her tent-mate, that she felt nauseated. She also had chills, a headache, and her whole body ached, especially her back. Her teammates took her temperature and it was normal, but her pulse was 105 beats per minute, far above the usual 60. They gave her Advil and took a close look at her big toe. They noticed that it looked much worse than it had the previous night and an angry red streak now stretched from toe to knee. Jen also said the lymph node in her groin was swollen. As the evening progressed, her nausea and chills went away, and then returned. The other students monitored her vitals, watching her pulse drop slightly and her temperature increase to 100 degrees.

John, the small-group leader, told me they'd read through all their first-aid material and had decided Jen was sick enough to need immediate help. They had only come in a pair because they wanted to leave Mark behind to provide first aid, and Janet had a slightly sprained ankle, so she would have slowed them down. John also thought Janet's presence would comfort Jen. "We decided we were just going to be two people, we were going to be fast, and we were going to scream the whole way," he said. John handed me some notes detailing Jen's vitals, a brief description of her symptoms, and a map marked with their camp's location.

It sounded like her toe infection had gone rogue. It had turned systemic: the poison branching out through her whole body. I was surprised to hear it was her big toe causing all the trouble because I'd been monitoring the infection she had on a smaller toe and hadn't noticed any other. My first thought was to hike the three or so hours back to their camp and give Jen the oral antibiotics we were carrying. But after discussing the situation a little more with Linda and Frank, we decided that the red streaking and swollen lymph nodes indicated that this infection was serious enough to call the NOLS branch in Whitehorse on the satellite phone. We wanted to inform them of the situation and get their advice. I was worried, but I felt sure we could prevent the situation from worsening. I grabbed the satellite phone and made the connection to the branch office. Once I'd relayed all the relevant information to the branch they told me to call back in 15 minutes to give them time to consult a doctor and devise a plan. We began to prepare our gear to head back six miles to Jen's camp for the night so we could treat her with antibiotics, in case that was the branch's recommendation. The more I thought about Jen's situation, though, the more I realized we would likely need a helicopter to fly her to Dawson City for medical treatment.

When I spoke with the branch the second time, they told me a helicopter was on standby in Dawson and the doctor had told them that, if the symptoms were accurate, it was a serious situation and we should try to get her to a hospital immediately. Before sending a helicopter costing thousands of dollars, however, the branch had some questions. Realizing most of our students were 16 to 17 years old with limited first-aid training, they were concerned whether their medical assessment of Jen's condition was accurate. They wondered if they could have misread some of her symptoms and that perhaps she was coming down with the flu instead. They were also concerned about how the students at camp would react to a helicopter landing next to them without instructors present to help safely signal the best area to land.

Knowing the students involved and referring to the meticulous notes Mark had kept on Jen's condition, I assured them I was confident with their assessment. Mark, at 16, was the youngest member of our expedition, but he was mature and academically gifted. As a high school sophomore, he was already taking university-level courses, including pharmacology. He had tracked Jen's vitals and had written a detailed note describing her condition and their campsite location. He had also figured out the longitude and latitude from the map, which is difficult to deduce even for most NOLS instructors, and we hadn't yet taught the students to read longitude and latitude. He had also given a clear description of their campsite, detailing a good location nearby to land a helicopter. During our first-aid and emergency procedures class, we emphasized the importance of writing everything down but we didn't expect such high-quality note taking. John said Mark had also been furiously reading the *Medicine for Mountaineering* in-depth first-aid book they were carrying to find out exactly what was wrong with Jen. I was also confident the students would have no problem with a helicopter landing near their tent. Unlike most NOLS courses in Alaska and the Yukon, which use float or bush planes to drop off rations, this particular course in the Ogilvie Mountains required helicopters because of the challenging terrain. The students had already experienced two helicopter landings and takeoffs.

Burning Up and Burning Out

Meanwhile, over at Jen's camp, Janet and Mark were caring for their patient as best they could. By 8:30 p.m., Jen's temperature had risen slowly. She told Janet and Mark that her whole body ached, particularly her head. She was also cold, despite being wrapped up in a sleeping bag, yet when Janet held a cool, soaked bandage to Jen's forehead, it burned hot within minutes.

......

Around 10 p.m., over the satellite phone, the branch director finally agreed to authorize the helicopter rescue. With a hefty price tag of more than $1,000 an hour, the decision to activate a helicopter rescue is not taken lightly. They were concerned that all our information on Jen's condition had come from the evaluation of a 16-year-old student. They also wanted to confirm the urgency of evacuating Jen with a doctor based on her symptoms. It would have been an awful waste of money and resources if we sent a helicopter to retrieve Jen and she had a simple localized infection on her toe. But now time was of the essence. Not only was Jen becoming very sick as the infection progressed through her bloodstream but twilight was also falling and it would soon be dark. The rescue helicopter couldn't fly without light. As a plan B, the branch wanted two leaders to go to Jen's camp in case the helicopter couldn't make it. John and Marlene led Frank and me back to their camp. Linda stayed behind to valiantly plow through the paperwork alone. We still had a second student group out traveling the area on their own, so it was important for an instructor to stay in camp in case they too had an emergency and came looking for assistance.

As we sped through the darkening wilderness, we were on high alert for the sound of a helicopter and we kept close watch for grizzlies. After a few hours, despite the long sunlight that sweeps the area this time of year, darkness arrived. And still no sign of a helicopter. I tried to stay positive. I told myself there was a chance the helicopter could have come from the opposite direction and we just hadn't heard it.

· · · · · ·

At 10 p.m. over at Jen's camp, things were getting worse. Janet was growing increasingly frightened for Jen. She had no idea if Marlene and John had found the instructors and, even if they had, whether or not they had been able to send for help fast enough to match Jen's rapidly deteriorating health. Usually strong and stoic, Jen had now broken down and was in tears. No one had ever seen her cry before. She was begging to go home and complaining of a terrible pain in her toe that felt as though she was being stabbed with razor blades. Janet was feeling more and more helpless, yet without antibiotics all she could do was sit by Jen and comfort her. Jen's temperature was now 101.6 degrees.

Later, Janet wrote in her journal:

I was scared and felt helpless because there was nothing I could do to help her feel better. She asked if I thought someone would arrive tonight. I said yes and hoped to God I was right, but I truly wasn't sure.

Then, at 10:30 p.m. I heard what sounded like a helicopter in the distance. After listening for a minute I quietly signaled Mark.

Another minute later, Jen heard it too. I didn't want to get her hopes up, maybe it wasn't for her. When I looked outside, I watched it fly past and my heart sank. Then it skipped a beat as I saw the helicopter suddenly turn around and begin to approach. I told Jen that help was coming and she started to cry with relief.

Sixteen-year-old Mark jumped out of the tent and immediately directed the pilot to the landing area. He self-assuredly slashed a hand across his throat to signal the pilot to cut the engines. He and Janet were surprised and excited to see the helicopter. As the systemic infection had gripped Jen's body, so had their realization that she was dangerously sick and there was nothing more that could be done for her at their camp. They expected one of the instructors and a doctor or nurse to be in the helicopter but the pilot was alone. They quickly gathered Jen's backpack and belongings and were relieved to see her, dazed but determined, walk to the helicopter. Mark gave the pilot her latest vitals and a note for the doctor. They said goodbye and watched her take off.

As John, Marlene, Frank, and I slogged toward the camp, the students were becoming visibly exhausted. Not only had they already undergone a full day of hiking but they had also run for three hours to reach us. It was 12:30 a.m. and they were still going. At around 1:30 a.m., we clambered up the large mountain pass covered in loose boulders that led to their camp. We had only two headlamps between us, so the going was slow. Because there's so much daylight in the Yukon during the summer, a flashlight is rarely needed so, to save weight, we usually pack only a few for the entire group. Thankfully, headlamps have improved in the last several years, and are no longer cumbersome to pack. Around 2 a.m., we arrived at the camp. Now thoroughly exhausted myself, I desperately hoped that the helicopter had picked up Jen. We called out, "HELLO! Is Jen still here?" Janet and Mark woke up and told us the helicopter had made it in and she was headed for Dawson. Extremely relieved, I thanked them and told them they had done a great job. I suggested we talk in the morning and in the meantime try to get some much-needed sleep.

......

By the time Jen reached Dawson City nursing station, her temperature was over 104 degrees. Once the staff examined her, they determined that she was dangerously sick and needed to be moved to a larger hospital in Whitehorse, the Yukon Territory capital. As Whitehorse is about a 13-hour drive, they called the private medical evacuation jet to collect her.

......

The next morning at camp, Frank and I talked with Janet and Mark to hear their full story. We praised them for doing such a great job taking care of Jen, pooling their skills as a group, and drawing from what they'd learned during the expedition. Frank and I then rushed back to our old camp, where Linda had nearly finished the evaluations and was waiting for us. We had one more campsite to hike to and we needed to keep the course on track.

The helicopter lands to re-ration our supplies. *Shawn Stratton*

Two days later, both student groups successfully finished their small-group expedition, with one group oblivious to the drama that had unfolded over the last few days. As we explained the situation to the group, they were all concerned for Jen. The next day, our scheduled pick-up at the edge of the Dempster Highway arrived on time and we headed back to Whitehorse and the NOLS branch, eager to find out about Jen's condition.

Connecting the Dots

One thing had been seriously troubling me throughout this experience. I've had students with tricky blister situations in the past—just take the poor guy on the Mexico expedition—but I'd never had a student's situation escalate as quickly and dramatically as Jen's, especially considering her feet had been checked and monitored daily. As the course leader, I kept turning the details over in my mind. I felt responsible. *What could I have done differently? How did this blister get so bad so quickly? Why had the infection spread so rapidly? What had I missed?*

As the group traveled in the van back to Whitehorse, Jen's illness was understandably the topic of conversation. For the young students directly involved in the drama—Janet, Mark, John, and Marlene—it had been a terrifying, exhilarating, and life-changing experience. And all the other students were clamoring for details. Thoughtfully, Jen had written a letter from her hospital bed and had it sent to the van driver so we could get the latest on her recovery:

Dear Friends,

How does one adequately express true thankfulness? Four of you literally saved my life. By the time I arrived in Dawson my temperature was up past 104 degrees. Everyone keeps telling me what a lucky girl I am. I came in at just the right time. Apparently I have bacteria in my blood stream (bad! Eek), which could have gone to my kidneys (leading to kidney failure) and my heart (leading to heart arrhythmia or heart attack. Double eek!). But thanks to the four of you, who ignored my stubbornness and knew something was wrong, I am going to be just fine.

I'm getting all sorts of wonderful drugs for the infections, so they think after four more days or so I should be able to leave. Lucky me, a month on the NOLS diet and now hospital food!

My spirits are high (that is when I'm feeling well), and I really wish I could have finished the trip with you all. But hey, I got a helicopter tour of the Yukon! And two ambulances all to myself, plus, they flew in a small medical airplane to fly me to the hospital in Whitehorse—not bad! At least I will have some exciting stories to tell.

So once again, thank you John and Marlene for making the trek to the instructors when I know you must have been tired, thank you Janet for reading to me in the tent and keeping cold bandanas on my head and reassuring me that I was going to be OK, and thank you Mark for being so ridiculously smart about medicine and making me feel like I was in good hands. You four have no idea how grateful I am for your kindness. I will never forget you.

P.S. My toe keeps growing in size and pus is finally starting to emerge, cool! (I had told Janet she should just cut it off with her pocket knife.)

We were all happy to hear Jen was doing so well, but I was mortified that the incident had happened. One of my students came extremely close to suffering kidney failure, heart arrhythmia, or a heart attack. The next step was death. Jen had barely dodged that bullet.

I was still racking my brains, looking for answers, when one of the group members casually mentioned something that might have seemed irrelevant, but eventually made everything fall into place.

"Jen told me she was being treated for anorexia up to two months before the course started."

I was floored. This information hadn't been detailed in the extensive medical form all NOLS students have to fill out. Before going on courses, students must have medical examinations and they must be out of any physical or mental treatment programs for at least a year. Jen herself hadn't mentioned anything to me, Frank, or Linda. I knew she was a vegan and not a big eater but I had no idea she had battled anorexia.

Back at the hospital, the doctors had discovered that Jen's protein levels were near zero and her immune system seriously compromised. When I heard this, it was an "Aha" moment of realization. They also said the infection had originated from a blister caused by an ingrown toenail. I was a little relieved to hear this, because I was sure the blisters I was treating on her other toes were doing well when I examined them before the small-group expedition. The whole time we'd been hiking together, Jen had never complained of any pain in her big toe.

As the lead instructor of the course, I felt terrible that I hadn't picked up on Jen's food issues. The conditions we were living and traveling in, combined with her weakened immune system, had given the infection everything it needed to spread like wildfire. Now that I understood why her infection was so severe, I racked my brain again, this time to determine if there had been any clues Jen wasn't eating properly. I wondered if there was anything I could have done to change the circumstances. It had been only 48 hours from the time Jen first left for the student expedition to the time the helicopter had picked her up.

Jen was in the hospital for five days. She was released the day we returned to Whitehorse. Jen was healthy, but with a bill of $30,000 in helicopter, air ambulance, and medical costs to show for the experience, most of which would be covered by insurance. That's a reason no one's allowed on these expeditions without medical insurance.

Jen, along with her parents, who had flown in from Minnesota, met with our group at the NOLS branch office. As she spoke with the other students about her ordeal, I chatted with her mother. I wanted to bring up the anorexia issue, but Jen was over 18 and it wasn't my place. A few minutes into our conversation, however, Jen's mother broached the subject herself, telling me about the treatment Jen had been receiving. I didn't know the whole story of course, but I couldn't help feeling frustrated. I knew that, given Jen's recent experience battling an eating disorder, she should never have been allowed on a NOLS course.

Being Brave

Jen's story highlights the importance of bringing your best self to a team situation, especially when you're navigating challenging or unknown territory. Jen was a fantastic student: athletic, smart, hard-working, and determined, but she had overestimated her own physical abilities. Her story is a lesson in knowing the time to speak up when you're in pain or a tough situation. Being brave is only wise to a point and there's nothing wrong with asking your teammates for help. In fact, having already omitted her health issues on her application, the wisest thing Jen could have done would have been to talk to an instructor early in the trip about her eating disorder. That way we could have been vigilant in making sure she was getting enough protein. At the very least, we would have monitored her more closely. Once the situation did escalate, however, Jen handled it with grace, and her teammates rose to her aid.

One of the greatest lessons NOLS students learn on a course, specifically during their small-group expedition, is how to use good judgment in risk management situations. We'd set the guideline that students must travel in groups of four (or three, in an emergency) in grizzly bear country. But it's impossible to have a rule for every eventuality, particularly when traveling the back-country. So I was thrilled that Jen's group had made the executive decisions they had in the heat of the moment. They used good judgment and common sense, which helped get the helicopter in before nightfall, thus saving her life.

Of course, Jen couldn't have known her failure to disclose her eating disorder would lead to such a disaster; she probably wholeheartedly thought she was up for the challenge of an expedition. She was certainly a strong hiker and smart outdoorswoman. But failure to disclose relevant information on NOLS applications nearly always leads to some problem for the student, and, of course, their teammates, during an expedition.

Since my experience with Jen, I've had other students who had eating disorders and didn't disclose them. On one occasion a student with bulimia was stealing food at night and bingeing. On an expedition, there's only so much food to go around, so stealing food can turn a group mutinous fast. I've also had to deal with smokers who claimed to have been "quit" for months, but in reality had only stopped smoking a day or so before the expedition. Traveling with someone, on an expedition, suffering nicotine withdrawal can be extremely challenging. Some people wildly exaggerate their fitness levels on the application form. In good faith they plan on getting into shape in time for the beginning of the expedition, but then they don't quite get around to it and end up having difficulty with the physical demands.

And then there's the story of the only student I ever had to expel from a course: another situation caused by a failure to disclose information. A seemingly innocuous omission in disclosure by the student led to the absolute hardest leadership expedition I have ever experienced.

Lesson: Disclosure

To be a true team player it's important to disclose any issues, personal or professional, that might impact your group. The success of your team relies on you to perform your role to the best of your ability, and if something could threaten that performance, your companions need to know about it to avoid a potentially confusing, detrimental, or dangerous situation. Jen's failure to disclose her eating disorder almost caused a seemingly simple annoyance, a blister, to turn fatal. Trust the strength of your teammates and fess up if you have to. You never know, they just might be able to provide help and support.

Have you given your team the chance to offer full disclosure?

FACING TEAM DESTRUCTION IN BAJA

Photo: Kelly Slivka

CHAPTER 4

I ALWAYS SAID I WOULD NEVER LEAD A NOLS SEMESTER in beautiful Baja, Mexico.

The Baja Peninsula, flanked by the Pacific Ocean to the west and the Sea of Cortez to the east, may be lovely, but it doesn't offer the sort of challenging course conditions that first attracted me to NOLS expeditions. By now it's clear that I thrive on teaching through overcoming adversity and extreme challenges. The Baja course does present problems like lack of water and relentless heat, but generally the northern courses like the Yukon or Alaska are more challenging. That a Baja student could spend three months on a NOLS expedition and never camp in the rain always bothered me. When it comes to leadership instruction, the idea of mentoring students excited about roughing it in the middle of Alaska or the Yukon is much more appealing. Students who select the Baja courses are often stereotyped, perceived as picking the course because they think it will be an easy way to get college credit while hanging out on sunny beaches.

At the time, I was employed with NOLS to split half the year working in student recruitment at the headquarters in Lander, Wyoming, and the other half out in the field instructing courses. Because courses aren't continuous, it was a challenge to fill in my required field weeks, so that year it made sense for me to accept a three-month-long proctoring expedition.

All NOLS instructors have particular strengths. Some are wizards at natural history, some have great sailing prowess, and others can climb the most challenging rock face. One of my strengths was teambuilding, and proctoring the ultimate challenge. I had also enjoyed and was proud of my first semester-long experience in Alaska. So when I received my field contract that year, I was pleased that I was offered a proctorship with NOLS Mexico in Baja. My apprehensions became a distant memory, cancelled out by the exciting challenge of another long assignment. I would be the only instructor to stay with a group of 14 students through each month-long section of hiking, sailing, and sea kayaking, while other instructors would come in to assist a section at a time.

I arrived at the NOLS Baja satellite branch in September, eager to meet my leadership team and prepare for the course. Preparing to be the sole constant instructor for a full semester always comes with a significant sense of responsibility. During our preparation, we work with a Program Supervisor, typically a senior instructor, who oversees each section of the course and coordinates events before and after we go into the field. The supervisor also supports us should we need help with a student evacuation or other emergency. Beth, our Program Supervisor for the first backpacking section, was a friend whom I'd never directly worked with before. For this section I also had two excellent supporting patrol leaders, Carla and Garth. Carla, a petite woman from Mexico City, was strong, both mentally and physically, had years of experience, and was a great role model for the students. Garth, the son of a long-time NOLS instructor, was a young, capable, and up-and-coming instructor on his second course.

During our preparation we had a meeting with Beth to review logistics, our curriculum outline, and risk management plans. As part of the risk management review we discussed how to deal with difficult students in the field. At this point I boasted about how fortunate I'd been with all my past students. I'd never had to expel anyone from a course in all my years working for NOLS. Granted, having students expelled from courses due to disruptive behavior is rare, but still more common than expected. I'd heard my share of nightmare stories and took pride in the fact I'd never had a really bad student or group. I guess, mentally, I was patting myself on the back at this point, attributing much of this good fortune to the passion, time, and energy I spend building solid teams early on in the course. I felt that if I implemented the right tools and worked tirelessly on teambuilding in the first week, I'd be rewarded in the latter half of the expedition with a highly functioning cohesive unit.

After all, this had been the case for all the courses I'd led so far.

Whispers of Discontent

The first week of the course played out as most do with students enjoying the honeymoon phase. The group seemed like a pretty typical collection of students: mostly motivated, fit, and eager, with a few possibly troublesome past injuries in the group and some overweight members, who might encounter some physical challenges along the way. Problems faced at the beginning of an expedition included the usual stiff muscles, blisters on feet, dehydration, and heat exhaustion. But the group was gelling well as they learned to cook and live comfortably together in the arid environment. Baja is a striking, wilderness-rich land made up of ocean and desert, with granite and volcanic mountain ranges stretching over 1,000 miles down the north part of the peninsula.

Around day seven, Carla, Garth, and I did a quick individual check-in with all the students and we then realized something wasn't quite working out. Nearly all the students we spoke to seemed positive and happy, but a common theme arose. A particular group member was causing problems. A student named Allen had managed to upset quite a few of his teammates. His cook group members were the first to complain. They said the tone of Allen's language was often antagonistic and that he wasn't even trying to fit in with the group; he often thought and acted for himself and not as part of the unit and seemed to disappear at just the time chores needed to be done.

Students on a day hike climbing a peak in the San Pedro Martir Mountains. *Kelly Slivka*

Until now I hadn't had much one-on-one interaction with Allen, but my first impression of him had been positive. He had immediately struck me as someone who wouldn't have trouble with the physical aspects of the course. He was tall, lean, athletic, fit, and coordinated. He could easily toss on his 60-pound backpack in the mornings while most students struggled or needed assistance. He had lots of energy, often running around and jumping from boulder to boulder and over streams, even when carrying his heavy pack.

Carla, Garth, and I had already noticed, however, that Allen often didn't practice the level of safety or judgment someone in the backcountry should follow. Jumping from rocks and ledges, particularly when carrying a heavy load, was asking for trouble. A sprained (or worse, broken) ankle in just one member of the group could have an enormous impact on everyone. He also had a tendency to wander off on his own. Wandering off, even for short periods of time, in dense forests crawling with snakes, without telling the team, was risky, especially in an arid land with limited water supply.

Carrying 11 days' supply of rations makes for heavy packs. *Kelly Slivka*

When traveling with a group in an extremely remote location, all risks are magnified, as the distance to medical care could be many hours or days away. Some students feel confined by the instructors' expectations: never go anywhere alone without telling the group, no unnecessary risk taking, and wearing footwear at all times. After the first few days in the backcountry most students understand the reasoning behind the cautions.

When it came to Allen's formal check-in, I made it a priority to get to know him better and to see if I could understand his perspective. We sat down and I asked him about his home life and background. He seemed willing to talk. He told me he'd spent most of his youth going from boarding school to boarding school and that his maternal grandfather was very influential in his life. His parents had met while his mother was on vacation in the Caribbean and she'd become pregnant. She was a single mother and didn't maintain any relationship with his father, who wasn't in Allen's life. I got the impression his mother parented from a distance because she spent a lot of time traveling.

When I asked him how things were going for him on the course, I carefully broached the subject of his behavior. "We've talked a lot about the importance of good team skills out here in the backcountry and how everything we do can impact the whole group," I said. "But sometimes it seems as if you act a bit impulsively. I realize life out here is massively different from the world you're used to, but you have to understand that if we don't pull together and help each other out, we all lose."

"Has someone said something?" he asked.

"There have been a few comments from your cook group. Yes." I paused in case he wanted to say anything, but he just shook his head, looking annoyed. I started again, "You've got to take on your share of the tedious stuff that comes with camping. The cooking, the cleaning. It's not fair if you disappear just around the time something has to be done. It makes extra work for your group. Also, you know our rules about always letting someone know where you are. You can't just take off."

"I don't *disappear.*" Allen directed a hard stare off into the distance. "I mean, yeah, there's been some tension with the cook group, but no big deal. Sometimes people are too sensitive."

"This raises something else I need to talk about. You might feel that way, but if a member of your group has an issue with you or seems upset, you've got to try and talk it through logically. There have been a few occasions where what should be a reasonable conversation seems to end up with name-calling and accusations. Is there anything you want to talk about? Is something or someone bothering you?"

"No… I'm all right. Everything's fine. To be honest, this backpacking stuff is okay, but I'm really just holding out for the sea kayaking and sailing. I'm really looking forward to that."

Allen seemed mild-mannered enough, but I got the sense he didn't grasp how his often-inappropriate behavior was affecting the group. I didn't know what else I could do at this point, so I went over the basic conduct requirements which NOLS sets out for students and hoped that some of what I had said would sink in. He promised to be more aware of his behavior and the effect it might have on the group.

The next morning we prepared for an eight-hour day hike from camp. We split into two smaller groups, a common practice when doing day hikes because it helps with teaching and learning; then we set off to investigate the ruins of an old missionary outpost. When we returned to camp, I learned from the other group that Allen had vanished. He'd walked off on his own on the way back. The instructor leading his group lost sight of him as he was hiking ahead of the group. The hike was not technically challenging to navigate, so the instructor believed that he would easily find his way back to camp.

I couldn't believe he'd pull this stunt so soon after our talk yesterday. Given our remote location, I didn't think he was planning to run away, most likely he'd decided he wanted some time alone. The navigation needed to return to camp was fairly straightforward, so I wasn't overly concerned, just frustrated. I'd never had a student wander off alone while hiking before, and no matter how capable and fit Allen might be, there were dangerous situations he could potentially get himself into. If he became lost or injured, the course and all the students and instructors would be affected. The group could be put in a compromising situation trying to rescue him, and the entire expedition schedule could be altered. Our location in the San Pedro Mountains was so remote it would take many hours, if not days, to reach a hospital. I refrained from organizing a search party, and kept an eye on the daylight, hoping Allen would at least return before darkness fell. He appeared four hours after disappearing, just before sunset.

The next morning, Garth, Carla, and I pulled Allen aside to explain how dangerous and foolhardy wandering off from the group had been. We told him that he'd displayed an astonishing lack of judgment and complete disregard for his and the group's safety.

"Allen, this sort of stunt is totally unacceptable, and also completely unheard of on a NOLS course," I said. "You *know* why we have to stick together, or at the very least let others know where we are if we leave the group. I've been over this several times. If you do anything like this again, we're going to have to put you on a behavioral contract."

Allen looked genuinely contrite. He acted as if he simply hadn't considered the ramifications of his actions. But he listened and said he understood, that he would try harder. What I didn't tell him yet was that being put on a written contract could lead to his expulsion from the course if he crossed the line again. I didn't want to get him too worked up at this stage. I was clinging to the hope that these were isolated incidents and he would get through the rest of the course. I'd never had to write anyone up before and I hoped Allen wouldn't be my first.

Several incident-free days went by and we became hopeful Allen had turned a corner. But before long, one student, then another and another, came to us with a complaint. The same issues: he was avoiding jobs, calling people names, and acting out. When I would broach these concerns with him, Allen would be receptive, talkative, and then insist he was being victimized. At first I didn't know what to believe, but before long I saw a pattern in his behavior. He'd instigate trouble with a member of the group, play the victim, and blame the situation on someone else until everything seemed to die down and then the cycle would start again.

Allen seemed to be getting into a heated argument with a new person every day. One evening I heard shouting and ran over to see him screaming at another student. His eyes were blazing and his chest was puffed up as if he was ready to take a swing. He was swearing, yelling "fag," and threatening to throw punches. Thankfully the student in question had the sense to walk away. It was as if Allen had no skills to deal with conflict and instead resorted to hurling insults and threats. It appeared that any disagreement could escalate to shouting, swearing, and name-calling.

Allen always seemed to apologize an hour or so later and things would calm down. The group tolerated his behavior at this point, but I felt sure something, or someone, was about to blow if the situation didn't improve. There was an aura of tension and strain constantly hovering over everyone. Garth, Carla, and I made plans to start teaching conflict resolution and effective feedback classes with the hope that it would give the group some tools to deal with the now-common heated exchanges.

From Bad to Worse

In my career as a NOLS instructor I'd experienced hardships, from dealing with broken bones, the threat of losing food and water supplies, and even the possible imminent death of a student, but the morning of day 11 of the Baja course was the most crises I have ever had to deal with at one time. We had just started letting the students hike for the day in small groups of five without instructors. This progression allowed them to build up the skills, judgment, and confidence to eventually hike for multiple days on their own at the end of the section. The latest group, however, had failed to return by nightfall the previous evening and now, come morning, there was still no sign of them. Garth assembled a search party and they set out early in the morning.

Knowing the challenge of navigating the terrain and that the students were equipped with the skill and knowledge to spend a comfortable night without instructors, I wasn't too concerned. I just hoped that in the light of day they'd figure out where they were or at least Garth's search party would spot them. My biggest worry was that we needed to move camp as soon as possible to make it to our next site in time for a scheduled re-ration of 10 days' worth of supplies. If we missed picking up the food and fuel, it would cause a huge logistical headache for our support team.

People were gathered for breakfast and I was scanning the horizon, willing the lost group to miraculously appear. At the same time I was keeping a side eye on Allen and another student, Jake, across camp. They were firing insults at each other and appeared to be on the verge of a fistfight. I was also worried about another student who had developed six excruciating blisters on each foot and might require evacuation. I couldn't see how he could continue to walk. As this was all running through my mind, one of the girls, Lindsay, ran over in tears. She was mortified because she'd lost control of her bladder in her sleeping bag during the night and didn't know why. I took a deep breath and tried to focus.

"Don't worry. It's easy to get the bag cleaned up. Maybe you're not well. You could have a bladder infection. We have medication for that. It's not uncommon."

"Really? It does sort of burn when I pee," she said, looking relieved.

At that moment we both whipped our heads around as the shouting from Allen and Jake suddenly escalated. I cursed under my breath. I saw Carla charge over to the warring parties, her face like thunder. Carla might be only 5'2", but she had a steely character and commanded enormous respect from the group, which was just as well because Jake at 6'5" and Allen at 6'1" looked like they were about to go at it.

"I've got to help Carla," I told Lindsay. "Grab your sleeping bag and take it down to the stream to rinse. I'll see about getting those meds."

I jogged over to the near fight Carla had already managed to diffuse. "Everything all right?" Jake and Allen had stopped yelling, although the silent glaring suggested that the disagreement was far from resolved.

Carla gave them both a look and said, "We're good. Jake was taking issue with some things Allen said to Meghan, his group leader from yesterday."

"He said women shouldn't be in leadership roles because they can't make decisions," Jake said with disgust.

"Yes, all right, Jake, we already established what you were arguing about. He's going to apologize to Meghan and you guys are going to keep out of each other's way, right?" Carla's tone left no room for argument.

After Allen and Jake had been sent off, I pulled Carla aside and told her about Lindsay's situation. "Do you think it could be a bladder infection?"

"I'd say it's likely. We should start her on antibiotics and see if she feels better. If it is an infection, she'll notice the difference pretty fast."

I was just about to head off to get the medication when to my enormous relief Garth's small search party appeared with the lost hiking group in tow.

It turned out the group had got back on the move again at daybreak and Garth's team had easily spotted them. They were fine and had managed to camp near water, a scarce resource in the area.

Okay, three out of four problems are somewhat resolved, I thought. *Now we have to tackle Matt's crazy blisters and somehow get him to the re-ration site.*

Just 11 days into the first section and Matt had developed six blisters on each foot. Some were several inches in diameter. I have seen a lot of blisters over the years but never so many and so severe on one person. Since the first day, we'd been aggressively treating them, but with strangely little success. It seemed Matt's hiking boots were way too small. Every day of hiking caused him more and more excruciating pain and we were now at the point of discussing evacuating him at the re-ration station the next day. Matt was an excellent student and team member and it was too bad he'd have to miss the last 10 days of hiking, but his pain level and risk for infection were just too high. He still had a month of sea kayaking and sailing to look forward to, and, if we got him out of the field now, he could make it back in for those sections. I just wasn't too sure how we would get him through the six-mile hike to the re-ration spot.

As it happened, Jake's six-foot, five-inch frame, which had almost found itself in a brawl with Allen, provided the solution. All the students carried two pairs of shoes: hiking boots and camp shoes (usually sneakers). We borrowed Jake's enormous sneakers for Matt to wear as we trekked to the next campsite. He was still in pain, but at least his swollen, sore feet could fit inside the large sneakers.

After 24 hours of taking medication, Lindsay's bladder infection symptoms had also improved.

The next day, Carla and I had a formal conflict resolution session with Jake and Allen to further resolve their disagreement. They had both calmed down and appeared cordial enough, taking the time to try and put themselves in each other's shoes. Again, I hoped this might improve Allen's behavior so we wouldn't have any more problems. Even so, we decided to start a separate written log on Allen's actions, which is something I'd never had to do for a student before.

During our re-ration at the new campsite we discussed Allen's behavior with Beth, our Program Supervisor. She suggested that we keep a close eye on him, and if we didn't see any improvement, to write him up on a written performance agreement contract. Before long, that was exactly what we had to do. Allen's conduct got worse and worse.

Carla and I sat him down and explained how serious the situation was becoming. We told him that if he didn't follow the contract he could be expelled from the course. Up to this point he'd never really got mad at any of the instructors, but now his defenses flared. He refused to sign.

"This is bullshit. I'm not signing anything!" Then he fumbled in his pockets and produced a business card. "I want to call my lawyer!"

I raised my eyebrows. It seemed odd that a 20-year-old would have a close relationship with his lawyer, or would have a lawyer at all, really. And why on earth would he be carrying around his business card?

"Allen, we don't have any other choice," I said. "Your actions are a problem for everyone here. You could put yourself or someone else in danger. We've been over this repeatedly and you say 'yes you'll change,' 'yes, you'll try harder,' but so far you haven't. Now we're writing down what our basic expectations are of you if you want to stay on the course. That's the process. That's the procedure. And we need you to sign it so we know you understand."

"I do understand. I'll change my behavior."

I sighed. "Yes, I hope so, but first you have to sign the agreement."

Allen's eyes narrowed and he shook his head. "Don't you know who my family is? I come from the Berg family from Berg, Minnesota. You know Berg Boats? My grandfather owns the biggest boat-making company in America!"

Allen's family history didn't mean anything to me. "Look, that's all irrelevant. We're evaluating you on your behavior and how it's been affecting the other students and the course overall. You've crossed the line too many times. Any other instructor would do exactly what I'm doing right now."

"This is a big mistake. My family could donate a lot of money to NOLS," Allen insisted. Carla and I remained silent. "Look, it will be different when we start the sea kayaking. I just find hiking really boring. I really came on the course for the ocean sections."

"That's great. Good to know," said Carla. "You still have to sign the performance contract."

Eventually Allen relented and signed.

For the next several days his behavior did change for the bet-

ter, but just as we would start to think he'd finally improved, another dramatic episode would erupt. A few days later, Allen had
another huge row that threatened to turn physical. He'd been
hoarding his cook group's juice mix for days. The powder was a
coveted sugar fix, a taste enhancer to improve the stagnant water
we had to drink. When several people asked him about it, he blew
up. This time the conflict turned into a battle between Allen and
Henry, another member in the cook group.

······

Later in the day, I sat Henry and Allen down to resolve the
fight so we could move on, but almost immediately they both
started shouting and talking over each other. It was impossible
to get sense out of either of them. They clearly weren't ready to
discuss anything. That night I wrote in the course log:

*I feel like a psychologist in dealing with Allen, listening about his
home life and having to write up every conversation we have. This
has been a major source of stress for me that I've never had to deal
with before on a NOLS course.*

I was now spending up to two hours a day just dealing with
Allen and, in the process, neglecting the rest of the students. I
wanted to believe I could somehow help him turn his negative,
disruptive behavior around. There was enough time left in the
semester and I held out hope that all this work with Allen would

pay off and not severely impact the rest of the students.

On day 20 it was Allen's turn to be the student leader of his travel group. I was not surprised when there were clashes with his team members all day long. I was mentally drained from dealing with the constant conflict. I felt like I'd exhausted all options in trying to help Allen become a contributing expedition member. That night I called Beth on the satellite phone for advice and support.

"I'm not sure where to go next other than separating him from the course with the strong recommendation for expulsion from the semester," I told her. "I don't know if the group can take Allen much longer. For over a week now we—me, Garth, or Carla—have spent at least two hours a day just dealing with him."

Beth was understanding and said she'd talk with the branch director. "Call back tomorrow morning and I'll let you know what we think you should do," she said.

To separate Allen from the course would be a logistical strain on the small support team. In addition to our course, the in-town staff were also prepping and supporting three other expeditions in the mountain range. Our nearest pick-up point was a long day's hike from camp and about a four-hour drive from the branch.

Expelling any student from a course is a big deal. The emotional, financial, and potentially legal ramifications could be far-reaching. If he had been doing drugs or displaying physical violence, it would have been easier to expel him. Disruptive behaviors are much more challenging to justify the necessity for expulsion. This was the main reason we kept a separate log from our daily course just for Allen. In some cases an instructor has separated a student with a recommendation for expulsion and for whatever reason the branch director denied the request and returned the student to the course. If Allen was separated from the course, I didn't want him to return. So I took meticulous notes daily. I even went to the length of having each student write a short note explaining how Allen's behavior was affecting him or her. I was shocked by what I read. He had negatively impacted all of the team to varying degrees. Several students even commented that he was ruining their NOLS experience and if he were to stay on the course they would consider leaving altogether.

The next morning I spoke again to Beth and she told me they had decided Allen should be immediately separated from the course. I was almost taken aback by how instantly relieved the news made me. I don't think I'd even admitted to myself until that point how difficult the situation had become. I never would have thought a student could push me to the point where I felt so powerless, unable to help him or her become a functional member of the team. That day the students were assigned a 24-hour solo experience where they stayed by themselves in one location, giving them time to rest and reflect on their experiences so far. Most students spend the time journaling or catching up on sleep. We were in a huge river valley so we set the students 100 yards or so apart in places where they couldn't see each other and arranged to check in every four to six hours to make sure everything was okay. Because of Allen's track record for getting in trouble, we'd assigned him a spot closest to the instructors. Once the decision had been made to expel him, we went and fetched him back to our main camp, then sat him down and gave him the news.

We were not surprised when he became extremely upset. He demanded to use our satellite phone to call his lawyer. We explained that the phone was for emergency purposes only. This upset him even more. He leapt up and started pacing furiously. "I can't believe this. I can't believe this. I'll kill myself!"

"Allen, take it easy," said Carla gently.

"I'm going to get you all fired for this!"

We asked him to pack up his things, as he would be hiking out to the trailhead with Garth and Carla in an hour. They were due to be picked up the following day at 9 a.m. My two co-instructors were both at the end of their section and I'd be getting new partners for the sea kayaking portion. Allen continued to rail against us, but eventually he had no choice but to do what we asked.

I was sorry to see Garth and Carla leave, but I wasn't sorry to bid farewell to Allen.

When everyone returned from their solo sessions, I told them Allen had been removed from the course and was currently hiking to the trailhead with Carla and Garth. They were all shocked and relieved to hear the news. I told them expelling him from the course was a decision only a director at NOLS could ultimately make, however, and there was still a slim chance he could rejoin the group.

They all agreed it was sad it had to come to separating Allen from the course, but they also all agreed it felt like a weight had been lifted from the team's shoulders. That night I wrote in the course log:

It really is too bad it had to come to this but I think it's the best decision for the group and Allen. I don't think I have ever been so emotionally drained on a NOLS course. I feel I've done all I can for Allen and with no change in his behavior over the last seventeen days I don't think a NOLS course is the right place for him right now.

Tough Decisions

The rest of the Baja course went smoothly, with successful sea kayaking and sailing sections on the beautiful Sea of Cortez. When I met with the other leaders back at the branch, I got a full update on what had happened with Allen when he eventually returned to the branch office.

Upon arrival, he had immediately called his lawyer. After speaking with him, Beth was also put through to further explain the situation. She was surprised and relieved when the lawyer, rather than giving her a difficult time, apologized for Allen's behavior. He told her that Allen had a troubled upbringing in the midst of a very wealthy family. He had already been expelled from numerous boarding schools and even a military college. NOLS was his last chance to prove himself. Allen and his family had failed to disclose this aspect of his background. If they had, he likely would not have been accepted into the course. At the very least, we'd have been better prepared to deal with him. Beth had a long talk with Allen about his disruptive behavior and then Allen had an even longer phone conversation with a NOLS director in Wyoming. It's rare for one of the directors to speak one-on-one with a student about a behavioral issue. As they talked for almost an hour, Beth, who was patched in on the conversation, became worried Allen might be winning the director over and that she might let him rejoin the course. Actually, the director was just hearing him out, and at the end of the conversation she simply said, "Thanks for sharing your side of the story; you're now expelled from the course. We can drive you to the bus station or we can help you with your bags to the sidewalk."

......

I still can't say why Allen behaved as badly as he did. And that's a tough thing for me to admit, as I am so used to making teams work under the most difficult circumstances. Perhaps Allen had some mental health issues; perhaps he just had a tough upbringing that left him lacking the coping skills most of us learn as we mature. People usually have reasons for behaving the way they do; however, a three-month semester in the wilderness wasn't the right place for Allen to work out his problems. At least I hope it taught him something.

Five years after the course I contacted some of the other students to gauge their recollections all these years later. I was happy to learn most of them barely remembered the details of their negative experiences with Allen and had only glowing memories of the course. I believe if we hadn't removed Allen when we did, however, their memories might have been quite different, and not in a good way. In an ideal world, every leader would be able to select his or her perfect team; unfortunately, it rarely works out that way. That's why I believe it's critical that leaders weed their gardens early, removing members who are clearly a bad fit or at least can't evolve into the right fit over a reasonable period of time. Otherwise the negativity generated by just that one person weaves a path of destruction that gradually takes down the entire group. Having the wrong people on your team can undermine the whole effort. Just one stubborn, angry, selfish student was enough to make that first section in Baja the hardest leadership expedition I'd ever experienced in my nine years working with NOLS.

Lesson: Pick Wisely and Remove Distractions

Not everyone is a good fit for your team. It takes a flexible and passionate group of people to thrive together and realize a challenging goal. As shown in the expedition in Baja, Mexico, the negativity generated by one individual can weave a path of destruction that impacts everyone else. If a team member seems to be a bad fit and you've exhausted all means to fix the situation, then ultimately it's in everyone's best interests to remove that person from the group, harsh as it may seem. A negative distraction might not necessarily be a person; it could be something else entirely such as poor physical environment or misaligned priorities. As a leader, it's your job to recognize when something's not working.

What distractions are hindering your team?

ABANDONED ON ICE

Photo: Shawn Stratton

CHAPTER 5

THE NOLS WADDINGTON RANGE GLACIER mountaineering expeditions are some of the most technical and remote courses the organization offers in the world. One particularly beautiful and difficult route is the immense landscape of the Homathko Icefield in British Columbia's Coast Range Mountains, Canada. Although, like all NOLS courses, no wilderness travel experience is required for signing up, this course attracts a different kind of NOLS student. Waddington Range students are typically more experienced, fitter, and stronger, both mentally and physically. Most don't just want to experience the exhilaration of a remote expedition; they also want to achieve set goals. Glacier mountaineering is an extreme challenge, no matter how much you crave the personal test and love climbing.

And it's dangerous. To move across a glacier, you have to travel roped to your partners, roughly 20 yards from each other, three

or four to a rope in case someone falls down a crevasse. Deep crevasses are common, which is why you also navigate slowly, sometimes like tiptoeing through a minefield, poking and prodding at
the ice around you. If one person on the line slips, the others have
to be ready to body-slam themselves down and haul the errant
climber back up. On a glacier, you can't duck out for alone time.
And, if you need a bathroom break en route, it's a matter of saying, "Guys, I gotta go. Can you avert your eyes?" You *cannot* untie.
At times, you can be stuck inside a small tent with several other
people for up to three days as a severe storm rages outside. Talk
about cabin fever. To describe it as an intense living experience is
putting it mildly.

It was the high-risk factor that drew me to the challenge of
glacier mountaineering at first, but it was also, eventually, what
led me to decide it was more the sort of adventure I preferred to
keep for personal time with friends rather than as an opportunity
to lead and teach. Stress levels ride high when you're an instructor
responsible for the lives of 12 students negotiating a beautiful yet
treacherous frozen wilderness. I'd wanted to work the Waddington Range expedition for several years because of the challenge
and sense of accomplishment it would bring, but also because I
wanted to experience the stark beauty of the area. I was thrilled
and nervous when I finally received my contract to instruct
the course. The goal for the expedition was to travel across the
Homathko Icefield while teaching glacier mountaineering skills
and climbing the nearby peaks. Although I'd been with NOLS

for years, I'd only worked a few mountaineering expeditions. I'd heard plenty of stories about Waddington, though, and was expecting my physical and technical abilities to be stretched to the limit.

I was excited to learn my fellow instructors would be Heather and Joel. I hadn't worked with either of them before but I knew Heather well from training seminars. A slight, but fiercely strong redhead, she worked mainly rock climbing and mountaineering courses. She was known as a great teacher and excellent climber. I'd heard Joel's distinctive laugh before I even saw him, and came to know him as a jack-of-all-trades talent who taught just about every type of NOLS course. He was a rare breed of instructor, one who was just as competent teaching white-water kayaking as multi-pitch rock climbing and glacier mountaineering.

We met at the NOLS Pacific Northwest Branch in Conway, Washington, in July, where I rallied with Heather, Joel, and 12 students to begin the expedition of a lifetime. Grinning happily, jittery, and full of adrenaline, we split into groups and made three separate trips in a small float plane that took us to an old logging camp at the mouth of the Bute River.

The Waddington Range course is so remote that float planes are the most time efficient and economical way to access it. Flying in a bush plane, although an adventure, can be disconcerting. I'm always nervous when it comes to landing, especially when the pilot shouts, "Look out for logs in the water!"

Our float plane leaving the dock on the Bute River. *Shawn Stratton*

As we flew into the Bute Inlet from the Campbell River, I didn't notice any menacing logs, but I caught my breath at the incredible landscape surrounding us. I could see many clear cuts scattered through the thick forests of the Coast Range Mountains. Squinting through the plane's windows, I caught glimpses of the great sparkling icefield looming in the distance, both enticing and intimidating with its prominent peaks, some rising up to 10,000 feet from the ocean.

At the logging camp we were greeted by a caretaker, who helped load our gear into his beat-up truck. He agreed to shuttle us up the horrendously overgrown logging road that would lead our way to the glacier, saving several hours hiking in mosquito-infested grizzly bear territory.

For two days we climbed steadily through dense willow and alder-covered vegetation, creeping slowly higher to the glacier, which was over 6,000 feet above where we'd started, at sea level. During that time, I encountered the steepest and most strenuous bushwhacking I'd ever experienced. There was no such thing as a trail. It was a relief for everyone when we finally scrabbled over boulders and loose rocks to emerge out from the treeline. Finally, we stood at the base of the icefield.

A student learning to ice climb. *Shawn Stratton*

The first eight days traveling across the glacier were ones of tempestuous weather. We faced driving wind and a rainstorm that forced us to secure our tent with climbing rope and soaked our nylon walls, forming puddles on the tent floor. As it was July, we also encountered broad blue skies, full of bright sunshine that bounced off the snow, creating temperatures reaching 70 degrees.

This sunshine was not necessarily a blessing; it spurred a rapid melt of the ice beneath our feet, opening countless yawning crevasses.

Practicing glacier travel techniques on the Homathko Icefield. *Shawn Stratton*

During this first week we focused on teaching basic wilderness/glacier living skills along with glacier travel techniques. We managed the occasional climb, too. We got to know each other well and I experienced what it was like to share a tent with Heather and Joel, two of the nicest, but messiest, people I've met. I was constantly amazed that it was always virtually impossible to find anything under the debris in our tiny three-person tent.

Heather and Joel were like two sides of the same happy-go-lucky coin; both full of the enthusiasm and passion that fuels a love for climbing and adventure. With so many challenging peaks around to climb, it was sometimes hard to focus on the technical logistics of teaching. Often Heather or Joel would spy an enticing mountain and bursting with excitement would point and shout, "I want to climb that! Who's with me?"

Dwindling Supplies

By day 10 of our 31-day adventure we were making progress, but we were getting low on supplies and needed to re-ration. We'd organized for a helicopter to deliver our next 10 days of food to the snow-covered rocky outcrop that was our current campsite. Our location was on a ridge 7,500 feet to the west of the highest summit on the icefield, Mount Grenville, which we were preparing to climb. The cost and logistics of helicopter re-rations in this remote area are exorbitant. To ease the burden on the school, it was imperative to do two re-rations together. The plan was for the helicopter to land near our current camp and drop off the first ration, then one of the instructors would jump in and fly with the pilot to the location where we wanted to stash our second ration. The instructor would dig a deep hole in the snow and bury the food and fuel. They would mark the cache with several three-foot bamboo wands topped with small flags and on the GPS. The pilot would then fly the instructor back to camp and pick up the accumulated garbage and head back to his base.

On the day our re-rations were scheduled to arrive, the weather was unsettled. One minute low clouds entirely surrounded our camp and the next a hole would break through, revealing sun and blue sky. Using our satellite phone we contacted the helicopter base and spoke to the pilot's wife to find out when we could expect our re-ration. At this time of year the pilot is often busy fighting forest fires and generally fits deliveries in when he has time or is in the area. She explained what we already knew: the weather was uncertain. She also told us a large storm was headed our way and that it might last four or five days. Helicopters are amazing aircraft but they don't like bad weather and above all need good visibility to fly. It was agreed we would call back after lunch and give a weather update at our location.

We ended the call deeply concerned and disheartened. A storm appeared imminent and we wouldn't get our rations for four or five days if we didn't get them in the next few hours. The large weather system moving in would prevent the helicopter from reaching us. We called a team meeting to let everyone know the situation. We asked the students to gather all the food and fuel we had left. As we sorted our rations, stress levels skyrocketed when we realized our food supply consisted of a few soup and oatmeal packets and spice kits. It wasn't much to sustain a group of hungry climbers planning to scale Mount Grenville, particularly several ravenous college guys. On these expeditions our packs are so heavy that we carry little extra food—plus we know we can survive for a long time fairly comfortably on soup. Because we are backed by a large organization, we're also never likely to be stuck for too long before receiving an emergency food drop.

Our biggest concern was our fuel levels. We depended on fuel to melt snow to make water for drinking and cooking. Without fuel we'd have no drinking water. We could survive weeks without food but only days without water. Different techniques can be improvised, like laying snow on a black garbage bag, but that only produces a minimal amount of liquid and wouldn't sustain a group of 15 adults. It also required bright sunlight.

With our remaining food inventoried, we scouted the rocky outcropping that was our campsite for any signs of running water. After about an hour, we found a small trickle that we could make work in a pinch. In the early afternoon, we checked in with the pilot. We decided that if we could see the sun, the helicopter could most likely land. He said he needed 20 miles of visibility to reach us. At that time the cloud cover was opening and closing, definitely not giving us 20 miles. The pilot told us to call him when the sky cleared and the latest he would leave his base to safely return before dark was 6 p.m.

Throughout the afternoon as the weather continued to fluctuate, the atmosphere around camp grew increasingly tense as the prospect of being stranded without food for days loomed. At 4:30 p.m. we could see more clear patches of sky. It seemed the weather was starting to break toward the north. We looked at our maps and tried to determine what we should be able to see with

20 miles of visibility. Not being meteorologists or pilots, we were woefully unable to gauge proper weather conditions for a helicopter. But by 5:45 p.m., the group was confident that there was at least 20 miles of visibility in the direction from which we expected the pilot to fly. In other directions there was nowhere near 20 miles of visibility. Knowing the poor extended forecast, we knew it was critical for our food to arrive before the bad weather hit, so we called the pilot, updated him on the conditions, and asked him to attempt the drop. He agreed, saying he'd arrive in about an hour.

Our food was on the way! The energy at camp shot up. There's nothing like the threat of food deprivation to send the spirits of a team of outdoor adventurers plummeting. As we waited for the helicopter, we cleaned up camp, tightened the guidelines on the tents, and marked the landing area with bright weighted bags. We decided Heather would be the instructor to fly off with the pilot to bury the second re-ration. She'd only be gone approximately 30 minutes so there'd be no need for her to take much more than a shovel and some flagging wands.

At 7 p.m. the group was overjoyed to hear the drone of the helicopter in the distance. We were getting our supplies! The pilot touched down on our makeshift landing pad in the snow without incident. He opened the door and tossed out five large green army duffel bags full of provisions. Ducking low, we pulled the bags away from the helicopter and Heather jumped in with a wave. A cloud of snow billowed up as the pilot lifted off and headed to the second re-ration location. The students frantically emptied the contents of the bags on a tarp to divide up the food equally into four cook groups. We had little time to reorganize our supplies before the helicopter returned to drop Heather and pick up the garbage. With the exorbitant cost of helicopters and fickle weather, we didn't want it to have to wait for us.

Helicopter delivering our re-ration. *Shawn Stratton*

Stranded

Ten minutes later, I looked behind me and gasped as I saw a wall of low-level cloud moving toward camp. I stared in disbelief, as within minutes we were totally socked in, the cloud engulfing us worse than it had all day. With snow all around and now dense fog, it felt like being trapped inside a ping-pong ball.

Heather was gone and we knew there was no way the helicopter could land in these conditions. Our visibility was now approaching 30 feet, a far cry from the 20 miles the pilot wanted. We waited another five minutes before trying to contact the pilot with our ground-to-air radio, willing a gust of wind to blow the clouds away. But they were heavy and showed no signs of moving. Eventually we reached the pilot on the radio. He and Heather were on their way back, having successfully delivered the supplies, which were now safely buried in the snow out of the reach of wild animals, namely grizzly bears and ravens. They'd spent a few minutes tracking a trail of grizzly bear footprints for fun, but then noticed the deteriorating weather and were now heading back to camp.

"It looks like you're completely socked in," the pilot said. "Get the juniors out of the way!"

Joel and I looked at each other slightly panicked. Did the pilot seriously mean he was going to attempt to land the helicopter in near-zero visibility? We were shocked, but moved everyone well away from the landing pad and gathered below a small rocky ridge. We could hear Heather in the helicopter. She sounded a bit queasy as the pilot maneuvered the aircraft, taking it to different elevations and approaches as he tried to find a hole in the cloud that could give him enough visibility to land.

"We're 15 miles out," the pilot crackled over the radio. "It doesn't look like we can get much closer. I might have to bring your girl back with me."

Knowing the forecast for the next several days was extremely bad and also realizing the enormous cost of helicopter time, we didn't like this suggestion at all. Another few minutes went by before the pilot came on the radio again. "We're 10 miles out now. I may have to drop Heather off."

Drop Heather off? In the middle of a glacier? We hadn't even thought of this possibility. Joel, usually so jovial, looked shocked at first, then furious. We clamored to respond, explaining to the pilot that 10 miles was too far away to drop her off without camping gear. Heather didn't have much more with her than the clothes she was wearing and a shovel. The threat of unseen crevasses on a glacier makes solo travel extremely dangerous. If Heather were dropped off she'd have to stay put until a rope team from camp could reach her. With prep and travel time it could take us 10 long hours to travel 10 miles, most of which would be in the dark as it was already nearly 8 p.m. We feared the danger that Heather and the rescue crew would face if we had to make that trek.

Finally, Heather came on the radio and we could hear her encouraging the pilot to get closer as she followed the GPS coordinates. "Nine miles… seven miles… six miles!" By this time everyone had gathered around the radio, fingers tightly crossed, cheering them on. "Four miles… Oh, it looks like I'm getting out!"

It was all happening so quickly. I wanted to shout "No! Stop!" But I knew the only other alternative at this point was for Heather to fly back and potentially be weathered in for days. Fortunately, before Heather had left camp, she'd grabbed one of our Motorola radios. At least we could still maintain contact. We waited, hearts in throats, the radio silent now as presumably the helicopter powered down and Heather leaped out.

Finally, we heard her breathless voice crackle over the line. "I'm out."

"Where are you exactly?" Joel asked. "Give us your location, Heather."

"I'm on a small sort of rocky island on the glacier… a little south from the large mountain directly to your west. I'm roughly four miles from camp."

We marked the spot on our map and promised we'd reach her as soon as possible.

"Heather, we're a bit worried about your radio battery potentially dying," I said. "Let's disconnect for now and check in every 30 minutes with an update."

"Okay," Heather said, sounding brave, but I thought I could detect a hint of nervousness. It's very rare for a NOLS instructor to be suddenly all alone in the middle of a vast and treacherous glacier. The team flew about gathering equipment to travel across the icy expanses to reach Heather. Joel and I debated which one of us should be the one to go. In the end we decided both of us, along with several students in two rope teams. If just one instructor had gone and then fallen into a crevasse, the remaining students on the rope, with their limited experience of glacier travel, would be in trouble. We hadn't yet had a chance to teach them the full protocol for crevasse rescue. We knew that the students staying behind at camp weren't going anywhere; they'd be fine on their own.

Darkness was fast approaching and by the time we set out it was nearly 9:30 p.m. Navigating with a map and compass, we left camp in two lines of three and four tethered together. As if on cue, the clouds lifted, presenting a calm, starry night and we hit our stride, making good time. The glacial ground beneath our feet was predominantly flat as we followed Heather's earlier instructions and headed on a direct course toward the large mountain looming ahead. After a few hours, we decided we must be within sightline of Heather's location. We radioed her to ask if she could see the lights from our headlamps.

"No, I can't see them!" Her voice carried over the static.

We flicked the lights on and off and moved around. "How about now?" I said.

"No, nothing."

"That's weird. We should be in the right place." We rechecked our location. "Describe exactly where you are again, Heather."

"I'm at the north end of the large mountain to the west of camp."

North.

"Heather, you told us south."

"I did?"

In the stress of being dropped off in the middle of a glacier with no equipment, she'd made a mistake and told us to head south when she was actually at the north end.

"It's okay, we'll redirect. It shouldn't take too long. Keep an eye out for our lights."

We headed north and within 20 minutes Heather shouted over the radio that she could see our lights. She sounded elated and extremely relieved. We picked our way to her location, our progress slowing as the ground beneath our feet became more uneven. Suddenly, someone's foot broke through what must have been a tenuous snow bridge hiding a crevasse. We froze, hearts racing. We stood in a minefield of crevasses, half covered or deceptively totally covered by thin snow. We kept moving, but our progress ground to a crawl as we carefully prodded the ground and navigated the treacherous terrain. Several people had more close calls, their feet slipping frighteningly through the surface.

A rope team traveling across the icefield. *Shawn Stratton*

Toward midnight, we finally got close to Heather. Shivering and ecstatic she darted over her rocky perch to throw her arms around us. She was a little cold and hungry, but delighted to have her teammates by her side again.

"I have to admit, I really wasn't ready to spend a night out here," she said, her face pale in the moonlight. "I was terrified when it started to get dark that you wouldn't find me."

We clipped her onto one of our ropes, all at once incredibly grateful for the close proximity of each person there. Turns out alone time on a glacier is overrated. Glacial travel, with its ever-lurking threat of falling into fatal crevasses, is an example of teamwork at its best. The purpose of any team is to reach a goal that would be impossible to achieve in the same way alone. There was no way for Heather to cross the glacier safely on her own after she was dropped off by the helicopter, but she was confident her team would find her and bring her back to camp. To make any progress, particularly in a risky situation, team members must be able to trust in their group; otherwise, all progress stalls. Furthermore, the team must be skillful enough to support the member in need. It's a symbiotic relationship and, in the case of glacial travel, is essential for basic survival.

With Heather clipped onto the rope, our team was once more complete. We left her lonely, rocky island, two lines of four now, and retraced our tracks over the ice to camp. We were ready to navigate whatever other challenges the next 20 days held in store.

As it turned out, Heather and Joel were destined to be a team for life. Shortly after our Waddington Range expedition they started dating, and today are happily married. I can't help thinking they must have the messiest house with the absolute best climbing walls.

Lesson: Expedition Behavior

I often sum up Expedition Behavior on a team as "doing your part and then some." It's about being the best teammate you can be, the teammate you would want to have by your side. It's doing things without being asked because you know they need to be done, or selflessly putting your personal goals aside for the advancement of the group.

As a leader or a teammate, is there anything you can do to improve the health of your group?

CLIMBING THE LARGEST AND COLDEST MOUNTAIN IN THE WORLD

Photo: Shawn Stratton

CHAPTER 6

AT 19,551 FEET, MOUNT LOGAN STANDS AS THE highest mountain in Canada. It lies in the middle of the largest non-polar ice cap in the world and, measured by its base circumference, is the most massive mountain in the world: 25 miles long, rising more than two miles above its surroundings. The mountain was named after Sir William Logan, founder of the Geological Survey of Canada.

My dream to climb Mount Logan germinated in the summer of 2000 while I was working at Strathcona Park Lodge, an outdoor education center on Vancouver Island. I watched a slide-show of a friend's mountaineering course in Alaska and was enthralled by the beauty of the glaciated mountain terrain. That evening, I determined to do one trip like that in my life. I had done some basic glacier travel, but nothing approaching a full-on expedition.

I felt it was going to be a landmark summer for me that year, as I watched that slide-show and sensed adventure taking shape for me in the future. I had joined just months before, taking the first joyful steps on my mission to become a wilderness educator. Those first few years, I worked mostly backpacking and sea kayaking expeditions, important first steps toward my goal. To increase my skill set I signed up for every instructors' seminar offered and before long I became competent in glacial mountaineering. Those missions, the challenges I faced, and the lessons I taught my students in every adventure supplied me with the awareness and skill set I knew I'd need when it became my turn to test myself on Mount Logan.

As I stretched my limits and dreamed of my next adventure, I found myself among like-minded people. I was no exception. I had planned and executed trips on my own to New Zealand, India, Nepal, Mexico, Thailand, and Guatemala but I'd never planned a personal trip with a team toward accomplishing a specific objective. I remember being at the NOLS branch in Alaska in 2001 and suddenly realizing that several people around me were in the middle of planning personal expeditions to some of the most challenging mountains and rivers in Alaska. It made me think about what I could do next to push myself.

At a 2001 NOLS mountaineering seminar in the Cascade Mountains of Washington I met Lisa, who was destined to accompany me on one of the most intense adventures of my life. A strong, slender woman with a big smile, Lisa quickly became a friend as we climbed and practiced mountaineering techniques at the seminar. Lisa was an extreme snowboarder originally from Minnesota but now lived in Crested Butte, Colorado. She raced snowboarding competitions at a high level and often climbed and then snowboarded off 14,000-foot peaks. As we repeatedly practiced technical mountaineering skills such as crevasse rescue, ice climbing, and avalanche safety, my confidence mounted and Mount Logan edged closer in my mind.

Later that summer, I met another would-be climbing partner, Kim, during a 28-day backpacking course in the Yukon. Kim grew up in Montreal but was then based in Whistler, British Columbia, where she worked as a ski patroller. She was one of the strongest, friendliest, and most easygoing women I'd ever met. Always looking on the bright side: she was a great teammate and (lucky for us!), a fantastic backcountry cook. I hardly even realized it, but gradually, subconsciously, I was assembling a climbing team.

Only a few months passed before Kim and I connected again at an Alaska instructor mountaineering seminar. This provided the specific information I might need to tackle a climb like Mount Logan. After the seminar I immediately started proctoring a three-month semester course in Baja, which gave me time to turn over details of the expedition in my mind. I hiked through the heat in Baja, envisioning how we might cross the glacier on Logan. One thing I kept coming back to was the importance of my teammates. I thought about what qualities they should have and I eventually came up with a list.

I decided they would need to

- **Be NOLS instructors**: Having familiarity with the same systems, routines, and expedition language would allow everything to run much more smoothly.

- **Have excellent expedition behavior**: A willingness to do their part, and then some. This is critical to the success of any team.

- **Have similar climbing ability and experience**: This would be an extremely challenging personal trip, pushing my skills to the limit. I didn't want to be teaching along the way, but I also didn't want to feel like I had to be taught or dragged along by someone with more experience.

- **Share similar goals**: With an expedition of this nature we all needed to share similar expectations and objectives.

- **Possess excellent risk management skills**: Our lives would be in each other's hands and I didn't want a cavalier risk-taker on my team.

- **Be interesting to talk to**: We could be stuck in the tent for long stretches of time.

- **Be committed**: There would be much planning, scheduling, and spending in the months leading up to the expedition. I needed people I could trust to accomplish the preparation needed. Many times preparing for an expedition is more challenging than the endeavor itself.

By September Lisa, Kim, and I applied for NOLS financial sponsorship under the Instructor Development Fund. This fund supports instructors' professional development. And, it doesn't just support expeditions; I'd received support previously for Spanish lessons in Guatemala and a Swift Water Rescue course.

Our planning continued throughout the fall and winter with me in Guatemala and Mexico, Kim in British Columbia, and Lisa in Colorado. We each had projects we were responsible for: researching the route, acquiring permits, planning transportation, ordering equipment, developing a grocery list, and on and on. When we instruct NOLS courses, we have the luxury of having the in-town staff take care of all these details before we even show up at the branch. It's unbelievable how much preparation is involved. However, for this trip we were on our own.

To research the route, we combed websites for trip reports and photos and interviewed friends who had climbed the mountain. Mount Logan is part of the St. Elias Range, an area with 20 peaks over 13,000 feet, notorious for hostile and fierce weather conditions. Turbulent systems in the Gulf of Alaska pound the mountains, churning up furious sea storms that can appear in minutes. The great sweeps of glacial ice can also create dangerously unpredictable winds.

We decided it would be best for us to fly into the Mount Logan base camp from Alaska even though the peak was in Canada. Most Mount Logan expeditions fly in from Kluane Lake in the Yukon, but we learned because of the difficult weather and high mountain passes, some climbing teams have to wait four or five days for clear flying conditions just to make the trip. Because the route from Alaska had no major passes to get over, the success rate of getting to base camp on time this way would be much higher.

Our expedition start date was May 7, but my own personal journey to the summit of Mount Logan started in Baja in early April. I'd just finished working a full three-month season of NOLS hiking and sea kayaking courses on the Baja Peninsula and would be driving my little red Mazda truck north to Alaska from there. This would be the third time I'd driven to Alaska in five years, the second from Mexico. Along the way I picked up Kim in Whistler and our climbing permit from the Ranger station at Hanes Junction in the Yukon.

The team finally together, preparing for the climb, at the NOLS branch. *Shawn Stratton*

We'd planned to stage our climb from the NOLS branch in Alaska. From there, we completed our check-in with the American and Canadian customs officials, having obtained special permission to cross the border during the expedition at a location with no immigration office (i.e., the middle of a giant glacier). Kim and I picked up Lisa on May 4 at the Anchorage airport and with that our team was united. This was the first time Lisa and Kim had met. As I made the official introductions, Kim laughed and shook her head at the craziness that, after all our endless meticulous planning and emails, we were finally an *on-the-ground* team.

After several days of collecting, checking, and packing all our equipment and food, we drove to the dirt airstrip in Chitna, Alaska, to meet our pilot and fly into the Mount Logan base camp. The flight on the ski-equipped bush plane was spectacular. We could see white snowcapped majestic, towering mountains surrounded by massive glaciers in every direction. To the south we could see how the mountains stretched all the way to the Gulf of Alaska. The flight in had given us a feel for how remote we would be, surrounded by hundreds and hundreds of miles of ice and rock.

Due to the often-intense weather systems that rage over the St. Elias Mountains and icefields, an experienced pilot is integral to the mission. While climbers might be waiting in the sunshine at their pick-up point, wondering why their plane is taking so long to arrive, the icefields can be locked down for weeks. Our pilot, Paul Claus, was a local legend. He'd been flying in Alaska over some of the roughest, most remote territory in North America since he was 13 years old. Paul was known for practicing unconventional flying methods, allowing him to accomplish almost impossible feats like landing on postage-stamp-sized icefield and even hanging glaciers. Because Paul was based in Alaska, he didn't have a permit or insurance to land in Canada, so he had to let us out at the border, a long six-mile slog from base camp. On the flight in he shared stories about the surrounding mountains from his vast years of experience and, when I asked him about Mount Logan, he said, "I hope you have your warm clothes, 'cause that's the coldest mountain in the world."

Our first view of Mt. Logan from the cockpit of our ski plane. *Shawn Stratton*

With that caveat, he maneuvered the plane toward the glacier. Savoring the last few minutes in the air, I watched the flat, white terrain stretch on and on, a great textureless mass with no variety. It totally threw off my depth perception. Just as I was thinking we were still several minutes from landing, a jolt and a cloud of snow startled me as the plane's skis touched down and skied along for a hundred yards before coasting to a stop. We quickly unloaded our supplies and reconfirmed our pick-up date before saying good-bye to Paul.

Unloading our month's supplies at the US-Canada border six miles from base camp. *Shawn Stratton*

Strangely enough, as I look back over the entire trip, I remember that moment when the plane left us was one of the scariest. As I watched the plane fly off, shrinking smaller and smaller through the afternoon sun, the enormity and isolation of our surroundings intensified. We were completely alone in the middle of an enormous icefield, the nearest road hundreds of miles away. The still air was total silence. We looked at each other, practically speechless. Excitement, nerves, and a sense of good fortune washed over me. We'd been so lucky with the weather, getting in on the very day we'd planned. We hoisted our packs on our shoulders and looked at one another. Our extensive preparations were behind us and we were standing at the starting line.

It took us a day and a half to travel just six miles from the Alaska border to Mount Logan's base camp, carrying our enormous, heavy packs and sleds. Although I had considered and weighed every item I had with me, I was in shock at the immense weight of all our supplies. We expected the climb to take roughly 21 days but, to be safe, we'd packed food and fuel for 30 days. Normally on expeditions like this we'd do two moves to shuttle everything from point A to point B, but the terrain was flat and we decided to try and cover it in one push. It nearly killed us. I found myself grappling with strong negative emotions as I labored on, wondering if I was an enormous wimp and more out of shape than I realized. My teammates didn't seem to be having as much trouble at all. I was relieved when I eventually asked them how they were doing and they admitted they were struggling just as much as I was.

Stunning views from camp 3 on Mt. Logan. *Shawn Stratton*

Base camp was extremely simple. It consisted of a few igloo-like walls that previous teams had built as windbreaks for their tents and kitchen. Other than a landing place for people flying in from the Yukon, base camp predominantly existed to give climbers a chance to acclimatize to their surroundings and run final glacier travel system tests before tackling the mountain.

Our most important system test was our self-arrest system. In order to protect each other while clambering over ice and crevasses we'd be tied together with ropes and harnesses. If one person fell into a crevasse, the other two would slam their bodies and ice axes into the ice to arrest the falling climber. Traveling like this is tricky and requires communicating by hand signals and one-word commands because it's often difficult to hear each other. It's crucial that each person on the rope team knows the system.

The first half of the mountain was a slow and steady, yet manageable, climb. Because of the weight of our equipment and our need to gradually acclimatize to the altitude, we did two carries per camp. On one day we would shuttle a load of supplies to the next camp, bury them in the snow, and then ski back to our tent for the night. The next day we would pack up our sleeping bags, tent, and the rest of our supplies and move everything up to our next camp. We did this several times over the course of seven days before we got to the halfway point of the mountain, King Col. When we left base camp, there were four other climbing teams ahead of us on the mountain.

The icefall we would have to navigate to reach the summit. *Shawn Stratton*

To our surprise, one of the teams was getting ready to aban-
don the climb. The other group told us they were thinking about
it too. We learned that the two teams had been stuck at King Col
for over a week, trying to find a safe route through a major icefall
that presented a treacherous blanket of open crevasses. We had
been warned about icefall by the park wardens and we knew getting through it would be the technical crux of the climb. Upon
arriving at the Col, I got my first good look at the icefall, and I
was awed and shocked. There were three icefalls in total. The first
and only one we could see looked like a 1,000-foot corn maze
angled on a steep slope. This would make for extremely challenging and dangerous navigation. We were hoping the teams ahead
of us would have already worked out a route through that we
could follow but, just 24 hours after we reached the Col, the final
team gave up too.

Leading the Charge

Now we were all alone at the halfway point. Just me, Kim, and Lisa: three young, fairly inexperienced climbers who were now the lead team on the peak. If other more experienced climbers had already given up, what chance did we have of navigating the nearly vertical maze of ice? We were prepared to find out. There was no way we were turning back at this point. We were excited and eager to take on the alluring and yet threatening icefall. The next day, we set to work.

Climbing through the icefall. *Shawn Stratton*

Lightening our packs by taking with us only the crucial climbing gear, we began to clamber up the sparkling mass. Despite the challenge of the terrain, I was struck by its powerful majesty. "If there is a heaven," I said at one point, "I want it to look like this. Although, maybe not so cold." We persevered for eight hours, getting shut down numerous times by tangles of crevasses, ice walls, and weak snow bridges. We gingerly tested the terrain with our ice axes and probes, eventually discovering a bridge that seemed strong enough to connect us to the next slope. We were thrilled! We had our route.

We spent several days ferrying loads through the icefall to our higher camps. We decided to go light and fast for our last three high camps, which meant leaving behind all our non-essentials such as our entertainment (a music player, shortwave radio, speakers, books, and cards). We also stashed a cache of extra food at the lower camp.

As we inched our way higher up Mount Logan, the most challenging part of the climb was the relentless weight of our packs and sleds at such high altitude. At times we'd be breathing as if we were running, but in reality we were only taking tiny steps, delicately navigating our way. Strangely, the intense cold didn't present much of a problem as we moved (we were bundled up to the eyeballs in the best, down-filled expedition gear), but dealing with cold feet in the mornings and changing in the tent was rough. We tried not to change clothes very often because there would typically be a layer of powdery frost on the inside of the tent wall and as soon as we maneuvered to remove an item of clothing we would inevitably end up brushing it all over our skin. Cooking was also a challenge. It took forever to melt snow to make water. One morning I tried to have granola with powdered milk and before I could get my spoon into the cereal the liquid froze solid.

Forced to travel into and over dangerous crevasses in the icefall. *Shawn Stratton*

Although you're part of a team during a mountaineering expedition, it can be a lonely activity. Most days are spent in intense silence, 50 feet apart on a rope. You spend a lot of time inside your own head. But when a storm kicks up, the team is forced to hunker down together in the tent, bracing the nylon walls against the buffeting wind. During this expedition, several storms forced us off our ropes and into our cocoon for six of the next nine days. We sorely missed our entertainment supplies as we hunkered down, held captive in our tent by raging weather. We went from isolated personal reflection time to intense claustrophobia and boredom. This is when having teammates with good personalities and a sense of humor is essential.

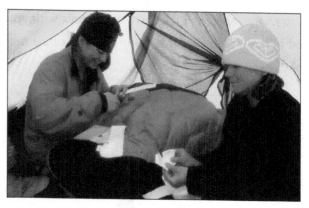

Making a deck of cards from a journal. *Shawn Stratton*

We got so desperate for ways to pass the time that Lisa cut out pages of her journal to make a deck of cards. Before we'd had a chance to mark them, she took a moment to duck outside the tent to pee. When she returned, she was practically in a state of shock.

"That was the coldest 30 seconds of my life!" she stammered, clambering back through the tent flap. "The thermometer is at minus 30!"

Lisa immediately set about drawing "hot" themes on the improvised deck of cards, so instead of the traditional spades, hearts, clubs, and diamonds, we dealt surfboards, suns, bikinis, and flowers. We also made great use of our pee bottles from that point on, determined not to leave the tent, for anything we didn't have to. We were in a high-end, three-person mountaineering tent that was comfortable enough for sleeping, but didn't leave much room for anything else. Because anything left unattended would freeze, we had to bring a lot of our supplies—boot liners, toothpaste, sunscreen, contact lenses, and most of our clothing—not only inside the tent but we also had to stuff it inside our sleeping bags.

Looking back now at that fog of days it's as if they ran in and out of each other to form one endless, cabin-fevered sentence. Few memories remain. Perhaps I blocked them out. I do remember at one point the three of us started talking about inventions that might make our life up on the mountain easier. Unsurprisingly, the main theme revolved around methods for keeping warm, like electric gloves. Another idea was a device to help women pee efficiently inside a tent. My favorite was Lisa's suggestion of a sleeping snorkel. At night as we breathed, a layer of frost would immediately form around the opening of our sleeping bags and the next moment we breathed again the frost would melt and drip freezing cold water onto our faces. All. Night. Long.

Mercifully, the weather broke and we managed to climb up to our highest point yet, 18,000 feet. That particular day wasn't just good weather, it was almost perfect: blue-bird clear sky, sunny, and warm at 15 degrees. We were almost certain the next morning would bless us with the same mild weather, giving us a great shot at the summit another 1,500 feet and six miles away. But sometime in the middle of the night a storm moved in, and I knew we wouldn't be going anywhere. The turbulence raged for two and a half days, the most furious weather we'd experienced on the mountain yet. Our spirits sank.

As we lay huddled inside, our disappointment about not being able to climb the summit gradually changed to concern as we feared that our tent would disintegrate around us, so fierce was the extent of the gale-force winds. After weighing our options, which were few, we climbed out, our bodies swaying in the turbulence as we set about building a protective snow wall around the tent. It was astonishing how much exertion the shoveling took at the high elevation. We were breathless and exhausted within minutes. Our tent was like a cocoon, a little safe haven. It's remarkable how a thin piece of nylon can protect you from such terrible conditions. It's also surprising how much noise it can make. Picture your bed sheets outside on the clothesline on the windiest day of the year. Then imagine those sheets are made of metal. That's the noise we had blasting in our ears for hours and hours.

So Close

After our second full day at our high camp our supplies dwindled and we knew the next day would be our last chance to tackle the summit because of time and food constraints. At this point we'd been living on noodles, soup, and Clif bars for several days. This is when I lost most of the 15 pounds I shed over the trip. That evening, the skies cleared up and the wind died. I was so hopeful that the next day would bring great weather for our summit attempt that I barely slept.

High camp on the summit plateau. *Shawn Stratton*

The morning of May 25 began clear, calm, and very cold (minus 30 degrees in the tent). The summit bid was a go! We were going to try to be the first people this year to stand on the top of Canada. Summit day would be an agonizing (everything at this elevation is agonizing) six-mile round trip, 3,000-foot climb (we would have to go up and down several other high peaks to get to the actual summit). This was the day we'd been saving our small chemical heaters for; we slipped them in our gloves and boots to prevent frostbite.

Several hours after leaving camp, clouds formed and engulfed us, severely reducing our visibility but not enough to halt our progress. As the clouds moved in and out, the wind increased rapidly and by 4 p.m. we were recording 40-mile-an-hour gusts. It had also been snowing heavily for the last hour. The visibility was deteriorating rapidly and it got to the point that we couldn't even see each other, even though we were roped together in 50-foot lengths. As the first person on the rope team I was doing the route finding, but in reality I couldn't see anything. We were in whiteout conditions. We decided to stop and talk about the conditions.

We huddled around. "What do you think we should do?" I shouted. The wind and snow obscured our voices and vision. My teammates looked like faceless bundles.

"It's not looking good," Lisa yelled back. Kim agreed.

As I was the leader of the group, my teammates looked to me to make the call on whether to turn around or press on. I was torn. I knew this would be our last possible attempt at reaching the summit, but the conditions were just so bad. Stalling, I asked Lisa to pass me her weather meter, a gadget that measured the barometric pressure, wind speed, temperature, and wind chill factor. Fighting the wind I held the gadget up as high as I could and squinted through my frosted goggles to see what it said. "Holy crap, it's minus 51!"

The past year flashed before my eyes, all the preparation, all the training, all the logistics, and all the money spent, and now we were potentially going to give up on our dream. It all came down to this moment. Kim and Lisa looked at me, waiting for my thoughts on whether we should count our blessings and turn around now or press on toward Mount Logan's peak as the storm raged around us. I wasn't optimistic about our chance to reach the summit in these conditions. But I wasn't quite ready to give up.

"The weather broke around this time yesterday," I shouted over insistent wind. "Let's push on for another hour at least."

Kim and Lisa looked at each other. They were silent for a bit and I thought they were going to disagree, but eventually they reluctantly consented to carry on. Kim took the lead on the rope team as we trudged upward. After just two minutes of virtually intolerable conditions and zero visibility I shook my head. *This is ridiculous; we've no right being here.* I tugged on the rope to get Kim and Lisa's attention and gave the turn around hand signal. They both nodded in relief.

Shawn, disappointed but relieved to be back at camp after the summit attempt. *Shawn Stratton*

So, about one mile and 500 feet below the summit, we called it off and turned back to camp. Physically we felt fine, but we knew we'd be risking our lives if we continued on. Fortunately we'd been placing wand markers in the snow every 60 yards from camp that allowed us to find our way back in the extreme whiteout conditions. We made it back safe and sound, exhausted and disappointed that we hadn't reached the summit but thrilled we were healthy and had not a trace of frostbite, which is always a worry. There were a few points over the expedition when I thought frostbite might be creeping in, but we always kept moving and were careful to use the chemical heaters for our hands.

The next day dawned clear for us to head down the mountain. This was going to be the fun part. The ski descent! I quickly realized, however, how difficult it is to ski in incredibly challenging snow conditions with a 60-pound pack at 17,000 feet. Wanting to carve it up and make some beauty turns quickly changed into *just get me down in one piece*! One good thing about descending was the speed. What had taken nine days to climb took eight hours to descend. When we got to the top icefall leading back to King Col, we were surprised to see about 10 tents and 25 people staring up at us. These people had all flown into base camp and moved up to the Col over the nine days we had been up high. And it didn't look like any of them had decided to make the ascent.

Lisa enjoying the descent on her snowboard with sled in tow. *Shawn Stratton*

Getting back down the glacier icefall proved to be much more challenging than expected because the ice was constantly changing and shifting. Not only were there bridges and cracks in new places but three feet of fresh snow for us to wade through. This section was too steep and technical for skis so we had to carry them on our backs. As we carefully made our way down, we noticed the people below had their eyes fixed on us. It felt strange to be watched. It was as if we were the evening show, although we must have looked like ants to them. For three hours we maintained our focus and tediously climbed down the slope. We were enthusiastically greeted by a crowd at the bottom.

Everyone was eager to know if we'd made the summit. They

were also full of questions about the route. They were disappointed when we told them we hadn't, but were full of congratulations for making it safely down through the icefall. No one on the mountain had heard anything from us in more than seven days. Some had thought we might have been swept off the mountain in an avalanche, so they were happy to see us alive. It was now about 10 p.m. and we were visibly exhausted. The other climbers immediately offered us soup, took our packs, and offered to set up our tent. It was a little overwhelming and flattering. I felt like a celebrity for a moment. They all seemed to know who we were and everything about us. Several of them talked about NOLS and others mentioned how great it was to see two women up there.

The next morning something interesting happened. As we slowly packed up camp to head down the mountain, several climbers from different teams dropped by for a chat. They were looking for route information and tips, but it seemed the main thing they wanted to do was vent about their teammates. I was surprised, and shocked, by some of the stories I heard. Here were some of the most talented mountaineers in the world and their expeditions were in jeopardy because they simply weren't getting along with each other.

One man complained his partner wasn't carrying the equal load and was in much worse physical shape than he had let on. Another complained his teammate had rushed up to King Col so quickly that he lost his vision because of the altitude and would now have to be evacuated. Another complained about his partner wanting to climb in what he deemed totally unsafe conditions due to a high avalanche risk. I was mostly surprised to hear these stories because Kim, Lisa, and I got along so well throughout the entire expedition, despite the fact that we hadn't reached the summit. It made me proud of our team.

After we'd given most of our leftover food and fuel to the climbers at King Col, we skied back down to base camp and over to the Alaska border to meet our pilot, who would fly us back to the land of the living (nothing lives at these elevations except snow, ice, and some exposed rock). Just before we took off, I asked the pilot if he would fly us over the summit so we could see just how close we'd come. He corkscrewed the plane up to gain elevation and reached for an oxygen mask: "I have to put this on because we're heading over 14,000 feet, but you guys don't need one." By now we'd spent at least a week living at a significantly higher altitude and our bodies were fully acclimatized.

Levels of Success

Many people say to me, "You must have been terribly disappointed not to reach the summit." Of course I was, but I can easily live with the decision because the summit was only one of our goals. Returning safely as better friends and climbers was a much more important objective. At some point we all have to ask ourselves what we're willing to sacrifice to reach our ultimate goal. And sometimes we have to know when to call it quits.

The purpose of a team is to work together to achieve a goal that's unattainable for just one individual. No matter how much combined talent you have in a group, it won't reach its full potential if you're not selfless in supporting each other. One of the most important aspects of getting along on a team and producing exceptional results is everyone doing their part And Then Some (what I call the ATS Rule of team building). On Mount Logan, a moment of revelation happened for me when I heard so many of the climbers at King Col venting about their teammates. Here were some of the most talented climbers and they were stopped dead in their tracks. Even though many of them had tremendous skill, their poor Expedition Behavior might well have prevented them from climbing higher up the mountain.

Sometimes in life, in careers, in adventures, in expeditions, all you need are trustworthy and dedicated companions to help you get where you're going.

Lesson: Build Trust

Developing and maintaining trust among teammates is a consistent lesson in every story in this book. Trust is the fundamental foundation for effective teamwork. Without trust there can be little meaningful progress toward fulfilling a mission. On wilderness experiences, trust inevitably develops quickly because of the amount of time spent together in close quarters and the often-risky nature of shared activities; people rely on each other for support. Trust is built through spending time together, being vulnerable, and learning the personal stories of your teammates. You may not be leading a group of people up the side of an icy mountain, but there are plenty of other less dramatic ways to get to know each other. Create shared experiences and discoveries within your group. Encourage people to interact, share, and have fun.

What can you do to build more trust?

FROM THE WILDS
TO THE REAL WORLD

AS I'VE CULTIVATED THESE EXPERIENCES over the years, I've tried hard to learn from them and put them to good use in various situations, experimenting and adjusting along the way. As a result I've been successful out in the field, in my career, and in my personal life. My hope is that the lessons I have learned will inspire and guide you too. Perhaps you'll be encouraged to finally take action toward planning that outdoor adventure of a lifetime you've been thinking about. Perhaps you'll decide to take a first-aid course. Ultimately, I hope the leadership and team-building lessons woven throughout these stories will help your own team reach its full potential and shape the way you lead and set examples.

These lessons have stood me in good stead along my journey transitioning from leading expeditions to starting my own company and building a career in the so-called real world—a place that can be just as scary, daunting, and exciting as heading off into the unknown wilds of Alaska. It's up to you to use these lessons in your own way, drawing on your own personality and strengths.

My Transition

Leaving a full-time career leading expeditions is a challenge for most instructors. It's a unique, adventurous, fulfilling job and lifestyle. We get to travel to some of the most remote and beautiful locations in the world and are paid to do what many people would love to do in their free time if only they had the money. Conversely, the career is incredibly demanding and all-consuming, and many of the uninitiated just don't realize the high degree of experience, skill, education, and leadership required to attain these life-changing experiences.

Adventure Travel Is Only Glamorous in Retrospect

There comes a time when the sacrifices which the lifestyle requires become too difficult to ignore. For many wilderness instructors, it's the physical toll on the body, the lack of financial security, the difficulty maintaining significant relationships with friends, families, and partners because of the constant travel, and the inevitable burnout those challenges can cause. When I finally made the decision to stop leading expeditions, it was due to a combination of all of these considerations, although the physical toll was the least of them because, thankfully, my body held up surprisingly well. I'd seen many fellow instructors struggle for years to change careers and leave the expedition lifestyle behind, attempting to blend into the nine-to-five, Monday-to-Friday desk job work culture. But after a few months away, many of them would find themselves back in the outdoors, leading another expedition, a job they knew and loved, but one for which they were gradually losing passion. I remember one instructor telling me, "I've been trying to leave this industry for longer than I was happily working in it." I didn't want that to be me. Starting off in the job, my main goal was to get paid to travel to incredible wilderness locations around the world while making a difference in the lives of my students. I felt that I had achieved that goal, and then some, and was ready to embark on a new path.

Throughout my years in outdoor education, realizing I wouldn't be doing it forever, I often wondered what the next phase of my life would bring. I think I've always identified as an entrepreneur at heart and I saw myself starting my own business some day. I was craving more stability in my life, not to mention a significant other. It's nearly impossible to maintain any kind of romantic relationship when, during the few weeks of the year you're not stuck up on a mountain or surrounded by hundreds of square miles of wilderness, you're living out of your truck or on a friend's couch. Once the feelings emerged it wasn't long before I knew I had to plan an exit strategy.

In the fall of 2005, after working a three-month course in Mexico, I decided to take the winter off and move to Vancouver to enroll in a three-month entrepreneurial studies course. This would be a structured (sensible!) opportunity to write a business plan and experience life in the big city. I had never spent more than a week in Vancouver, even though it was technically my base of operations, which basically means it was where my mailbox was located.

It wasn't long before I realized just how expensive city life could be. Unable to commit to a full-time job, I enlisted with a temp agency and was sent out to work as a laborer on construction sites. It was an eye-opening experience, a window into a completely different world. I mostly kept to myself, did my work, and observed the activity and conversations around me. All the while, I kept thinking how much the team of construction workers and especially the foreman could use some leadership and communications training.

In my entrepreneurial course, I stayed true to my expedition background and developed a business plan for an international outdoor adventure company. I wanted to take high school students on adventure education and volunteer trips to experience unique cultures around the world in locations like India, Kenya, Ecuador, and Newfoundland and Labrador. Once the plan was complete and the financial projections in place, reality set in. I couldn't just open my doors one day and have 10 trips fill up. I needed to build credibility and a client base. I needed to submit proposals to schools that might be interested. I also needed money to survive on while I was getting the business off the ground. It didn't help that I was living in one of the most expensive cities in the world. And after three months of urban life, the persuasive fingers of wanderlust tugged at me, making me miss the wilderness. As if to conspire against my small business plan, a few dream adventure contracts suddenly dropped in my lap and, even though I knew I should be focusing on my business, I just wasn't ready to relinquish the opportunities. India and Australia beckoned.

When most people open a small business, they often keep their day job for a few years until they're properly established. My problem was my day job leading expeditions meant I would have to be completely out of touch with the rest of the world for up to a month at a time. I tried to juggle my expedition contracts while growing my business, but I started to miss responses from potential clients to whom I had worked so hard to submit proposals and inevitably the business was put on hold for a month or two at a time. When I was able to promote my new endeavor, however, I'd conduct presentations in schools and travel stores to conjure up interest. I'd been doing slide-shows and talks about my expedition adventures for years and I wanted to become a better presenter, so I joined a local Toastmasters club. I was inspired to learn the craft of keynote speaking and enjoyed sharing my stories.

By 2008, I'd successfully led several American school groups on educational outdoor adventures to Newfoundland and Labrador as part of my new business. At the same time I was struggling to keep up with the high cost of living in Vancouver, British Columbia, so I decided to move back permanently to my hometown, St. John's, Newfoundland and Labrador. Upon returning, I rewrote my business plan and reevaluated what I wanted to do with the next 10 years of my life. I decided once and for all that I was burnt out from leading extended expeditions and I also faced major obstacles in the youth international travel market, namely the high cost of business insurance and a declining target market in the wake of a major economic downturn. So I redirected and intensified my focus on professional speaking, corporate team building, and leadership consulting—an interest ever since I worked with corporate groups during a college internship at Outward Bound. I thought that if I could successfully lead and teach groups on wilderness expeditions in harsh conditions 24/7 for weeks at a time, surely I had insights to share that could help corporations develop their leadership skills and be more effective in their nine-to-five world.

I've now successfully been running my professional speaking and consulting business since 2008. I have clients throughout Canada, the United States, and Europe and split my time between keynote speaking and facilitating team building and leadership workshops.

Before I left Vancouver, my friends asked about how I'd get my challenging "mountain fix" while living in St. John's. I'd emerged from almost 15 years living, working, and playing at a high physical capacity while thriving on adventure in the mountains and now I was about to live in a place called *The Rock*. Newfoundland and Labrador boasts some stunning outdoor scenery, but no mountains to compare to those in British Columbia, Alaska, or the Himalayas. Yet Newfoundland features plenty of water to swim in, roads to bike, and trails to run. Having returned to the place of my youth, I recalled my earlier affinity for triathlons. Feeling the familiar lure and promise of an experience yet to be had, I signed up for the 2009 Ironman Canada, a race I had dreamed of doing for 17 years. I had found my adventure fix.

I have since completed my second Ironman, this one in Lake Placid, NY. In 2013 I completed the storied Boston Marathon after achieving the qualification time in the St. John's Marathon, a long-term bucket list item made more meaningful by the serious events of that day. My heart goes out to the victims of the Boston Marathon bombings and their families, and my praise to the first responders and the spirited city of Boston.

I also found something else. In training for the Ironman and just a few months after arriving home in St. John's, I met the woman who would become my wife. She had also just moved there and was also signed up to compete in Ironman Canada. She has become my newest adventure partner.

My travel adventures have now taken a slightly different form because now we have a 21-month-old daughter and another on the way. When our daughter was three months old, my wife and I took her to Costa Rica for four weeks and enjoyed many day adventures on the coast and in the jungle. Just recently, we took her on her first overnight backpacking trip, a rugged 16-mile coastal trek along Newfoundland and Labrador's beautiful East Coast Trail.

There are days I miss my life on the road, and occasionally I feel my old lifestyle experimentally tugging at me, but I have no regrets about closing that chapter of my life. Fatherhood has given me a new perspective and a new way of thinking about the types of adventures I want to pursue in the future. I'm sure there will be many more mountains to climb, oceans to paddle, and races to run, only this time I'll be leading my family. And my passion for experiential education and inspiring people to realize their potential endures in my consulting practice.

ACKNOWLEDGEMENTS

I WOULD LIKE TO EXPRESS MY GRATITUDE to the many people who saw me through this book; to all those who provided support, talked things over, read, wrote, offered comments, allowed me to use their pictures and assisted in the editing, proofreading, and design.

I would like to thank my fantastic editing team: concept editor Clare-Marie Grigg for bringing my words to life, manuscript editor Casey Livingston for her attention to detail, and the final copy editor, Iona Bulgin, for her ability to do surgery on sentences. Without their combined writing and editing talents this book would still be trapped in my head and the stories fading from memory. I am grateful for the design skills and patience of Jen Moss, who designed the cover and book layout. Her commitment to seeing this project through despite my many "last edits" was admirable.

I would like to acknowledge my fantastic team of beta copy readers: Rob Briggs, PhD; Kim Larouche; TA Loeffler, PhD; Bob Miller, MD; Gavin Murphy; Paul Pearson; Bruce Piller;

Stephanie Porter; Rudy Riedlsperger; Dave Robbins; Ian Royle; Jerry Singleton, PhD; and Darryl Stratton. I really appreciate that they took the time to read the manuscript and offer comments and suggestions to make *TEAMS ON THE EDGE* a better book.

I also owe a special thanks to all the NOLS students and staff I've had the pleasure of working with over the years. Without their passion, dedication, sense of adventure, and commitment to stretch themselves outside their comfort zones, none of these stories would have been written.

Above all, I want to thank the most important people in my life. My wife, Alexandra, and my daughter, Sierra, whose unconditional love and support have carried me in so many ways throughout this project. My parents, Ed and Judy Stratton, who instilled the confidence in me to always follow my passion, and my brothers, Neal and Darryl, for their tremendous advice and encouragement. I love you all dearly!

Last and not least, I beg forgiveness of all the people who have supported me in this project over the years and whose names I have failed to mention.

Thank you!

DRIVEN BY A PASSION FOR EXPERIENTIAL EDUCATION and adventure, Shawn has devoted 15 years to leading over 2,000 days of wilderness leadership expeditions into some of the world's harshest environments as a senior instructor with the National Outdoor Leadership School and other international organizations. Along the way, his skill for fostering powerful teams has made him a sought-after speaker, workshop leader, and business consultant.

Building powerful teams through leadership, Shawn pulls from his rich experience and background as an explorer and consultant. Founder of the LiveMore Group, an organization that helps people maximize their potential and productivity, Shawn designs presentations and retreats for small businesses and large corporations. As a keynote speaker, Shawn brings energy, thought-provoking ideas, and a passion for team building to the stage. During his multimedia presentations, Shawn shares breathtaking photos, captivating stories, and valuable team-building lessons that are just as relevant inside the boardroom as they are in the wilds of Kenya or the Himalayas.

CONNECT WITH SHAWN

 www.facebook.com/shawn.stratton.79

 www.linkedin.com/in/shawnstratton

 http://twitter.com/SStratton1

 www.youtube.com/user/ShawnNMStratton

 Scan this QR Code to download my TED Talk or visit my website shawnstratton.com.

For free articles, audios, and videos 3-4 times per month, subscribe to Shawn's blog at www.shawnstratton.com.

If you want to receive an automatic email when Shawn's next book is released, simply email nextbook@livemoregroup.com. Your email address will never be shared and you can unsubscribe at any time.

Word of mouth is crucial for any author's success. If you enjoyed the book, please consider leaving a review at Amazon, even if it's only a line or two; it would make a difference and it would also be very much appreciated.

Lightning Source UK Ltd.
Milton Keynes UK
UKOW06f0704300813

216216UK00009B/14/P